FOLLOWING THE SHOALS

Cornerstones of Modern Irish Fishing

PAT NOLAN

The History Press Ireland

This book is dedicated to all fishermen.
May the holes in your nets be no larger than the fish in them! (Irish Blessing)

James McLeod, pictured on the front cover of this book, sadly passed away on 27 October 2010, at the age of 97.

First published 2010

The History Press Ireland
119 Lower Baggot Street
Dublin 2, Ireland
www.thehistorypress.ie

British Library Cataloguing in Publication Data.
A catalogue record for this book is available from the British Library.

ISBN 978 1 84588 990 6

Typesetting and origination by The History Press
Printed in Great Britain
Manufacturing managed by Jellyfish Print Solutions Ltd

CONTENTS

ACKNOWLEDGEMENTS

Researching the material and subsequently writing this book was indeed a great pleasure. The enjoyment I derived from meeting up with those who contributed was immense. The main content of the book came through individuals who willingly spent many hours in conversation with me. Yes, it was those men who answered my call and invited me into their homes who made it all possible. I extend my sincere thanks to each and every one of them. Special mention of nonagenarian James McLeod will, I'm sure, not cause offence. The general demeanour and clarity of recall ever present during my meetings with this aged gentleman were truly enthralling.

It would be amiss of me not to also mention John McBride. When I met up with him in 2009 he was in his eighty-seventh year and suffering from deteriorating health. Undaunted, John, with a smile on his face, talked incessantly and greatly amused me with accounts of his younger days carousing around County Donegal. Sadly, John passed away within months of my visit.

Help and encouragement with my last book, *Sea Change*, came freely from *Marine Times* newspaper editor, Mark McCarthy. This time around, his input has once again been invaluable and greatly appreciated.

Photographs are an integral part of this book. Accordingly, sincere thanks go to those who contributed so handsomely! Francis Cunningham of Killybegs, County Donegal, was a major provider. He also sourced several important titbits of information that would otherwise not have been forthcoming.

As with most projects in life, kind words, tolerance and support from those close to oneself are of the essence. During the research and writing of this book, my wife, Una, my son and daughters have each measured up beyond the call of duty on all counts.

When alighting from buses in certain parts of the country, youngish females thank the driver by saying, 'Thanks a million.' While the exact meaning of the expression eludes me, somehow I feel it gives a dimension in excess of the more familiar words of gratitude usually expressed. As such, to all those people who in anyway helped in furthering my dream of writing this book, I say, 'Thanks a million.'

PREFACE

In late 2008, my book *Sea Change* was published by Nonsuch Publishing (now The History Press Ireland). It is a compilation presented in two parts based on research personally carried out into the rise of the BIM 50-footer and its impact on coastal Ireland. The term 'BIM 50-footer' is widely used to identify a particular type of fishing boat, 50ft long, built by An Bord Iascaigh Mhara in the 1950s and '60s. Some of the book's content was received via communication facilities so readily available in this day and age. However, much of it was amassed during my visits to individual fishermen around the Irish coastline. The purpose of those visits was to personally learn something of the history of the boats, as well as to record the views of owners. It was a thoroughly enjoyable experience. I decided at that time to concentrate solely on researching the 50-footer story, but increasingly it occurred to me that sometime in the future I would like to focus on the life experiences of retired, high-profile fishermen in general, as opposed to those just involved with the 50-footers.

Encouraged by a few casual meetings with now-retired fishermen, boat builders and a marine engineer, I decided to follow my dream. My first visit was to a retired fisherman and absolute gentleman who again and again over the years had been described to me as 'a father figure' and 'the cornerstone' of the modern-day fishing industry at Killybegs, County Donegal, now widely recognised as Ireland's premier fishing port. The man in question was James McLeod. I was so well received and so enjoyed our chat that if a catalyst was needed to spur me on with the notion of talking to retired fishermen, then that was it! In the months that followed it has given me untold pleasure to travel around the coastline and listen to the recollections of so many great men of the sea.

INTRODUCTION

Following the Shoals is based on information sourced during fairly lengthy and pleasantly conversational meetings with retired fishermen, and occasionally with other individuals associated with the fishing industry. I soon realised, that based on their experiences, each individual skipper and/or boat owner had his own story to tell. The majority of those I spoke with began fishing as deckhands at an early age, many as teenagers, came up through the ranks to become owners, and updated their boats several times over the years, getting bigger and better vessels each time.

This book reflects varied experiences, opinions, memories, perceptions, fulfilments, grievances, disappointments, humourous occurances and occasional tints of sadness. Above all, it deals with the parts played by great and courageous men in an industry that, through no fault of their own, is generally perceived to have seriously underachieved as a national asset.

An added facet to the book is the inclusion of memories and experiences of a body of men close to the hearts of boat owners. That body includes boatyard men and those who kept the boats at sea through their marine engineering input. It was a fisherman who suggested that memories of those men should have a place in a book of this kind.

I see this book as an insight into what it takes to become a fisherman at the highest level, where courage, determination, astuteness, pitting one's wits against the elements, expertise in the use of fishing gear and modern technology, man management, adhering to bureaucracy and simply making a living are all exemplified.

A FATHER FIGURE AND CORNERSTONE

JAMES MCLEOD OF SCOTLAND AND KILLYBEGS, COUNTY DONEGAL

A miserable day by any standards! That best describes the weather on a particular late February afternoon in Sligo. It was the afternoon on which I had arranged to meet up with James McLeod at his daughter's residence on the Strandhill Road. Una and I were on our way to Galway. We arrived at Sligo earlier than expected and drove out to the Strandhill car park, where we whiled away the time listening to the radio and watching the strong, drizzle-bearing westerly wind whipping up the spray along the shore in the shallow waters of Sligo Bay. When the time came for me to travel the four or so miles back towards Sligo to meet James, Una stayed behind at a local hostelry.

My introduction to James came through his daughter Jillian, who had already warmly welcomed me to her home. Once I began to converse with the amiable and cultured gentleman that James McLeod is, all thoughts of the miserable day outdoors quickly evaporated. From the outset I was aware that this ninety-six-year-old gentleman had a wonderful and interesting story to tell. He had previously been described to me as a 'renowned ultra-progressive fisherman, a father figure, and cornerstone of the Killybegs fishing industry'. As such I knew this man was special.

James McLeod, 2009.

James, who was born in Scotland, began by telling me he believes he was destined to go to sea. 'It was in the genes,' he said. Even at school he had a strong leaning in that direction. In late 1928, he joined the Head Line Shipping Company, Belfast, on a four-year apprenticeship. Unfortunately, the completion of his apprenticeship coincided with the Great Depression of the 1930s and the devastating consequences it had on shipping. Jobs were very scarce. However, lady luck came to the rescue. As James put it:

> I got a job out of my turn as second mate on one of the smaller Dublin ships run by the Head Line Company. At short notice they needed a person to fill the post in one of their continental traders. I knew that I wasn't even in turn for a third mate's berth! It was obvious that the job wouldn't last. Decommissioning of the company ships was ongoing and as a result senior people were piling up ashore. Six months later I was replaced and that left me ashore with little prospects of finding another job at sea in the times that prevailed. Shipping was very badly hit by the Depression.

James was not one to sit around idle, and he had several ideas about what career he might follow. None of them immediately materialised and it was during that time, through a school chum connection, that he met up with Tom Swan while visiting Ballyshannon, County Donegal. Tom was then serving his time at the Harland & Wolff Shipyard in Belfast. Shortly afterwards he returned to Ballyshannon to take over as manager of Erne Fisheries, a company with rights to salmon fishing on the River Erne. The position had previously been held by his father, who was forced to retire as result of an accident. That was around 1934. Significantly, following Tom's appointment, a prolonged lawsuit ended with the fishing rights to the tidal part of the river being lost.

James didn't know it then, but the outcome of that particular lawsuit was to launch him on a career journey that would eventually not only leave an indelible mark on his own life but also on that of umpteen others who were fortunate enough to cross his path. It came about as follows: a 32ft clinker built half-decker, *Tern*, owned by Erne Fisheries had become redundant as a result of the loss of the tidal part of the river-fishing rights. Rather than having it lying idle, Tom Swan decided to convert it to a commercial fishing boat. That's where James came in, and this is how he recalls his introduction to fishing:

> Tom asked me if I would like to participate in the venture. Obviously an experienced fisherman would take charge of the boat. At the time it was an opportunity I couldn't afford to turn down. It was certainly worth pursuing, so I went to Ballyshannon. My first assignment was to overhaul the 12/14hp Thornycroft Engine that was fitted in the *Tern*. Then I discovered that we were not to fish out of Ballyshannon, but a place called Killybegs. I'd never heard of it! When all was shipshape I took the boat across Donegal Bay to the much more suitable harbour at Killybegs.

From that day on, one way and another, James was to be involved with fishing. With great clarity James recalls how events unfolded:

> Tom had arranged with a St John's Point fisherman to skipper the boat. His name was Francis (Francie) McCallig. Francie was a very good fisherman,

an intelligent and knowledgeable man, a man from whom I learnt a great deal about fishing, fishing grounds and sailing. We hit an extremely poor first season. For natural reasons the fish had deserted the area. Things were so bad that several boat owners right around Donegal Bay decided to tie up for the season. We struggled away, half scraping a living, but we were not well treated by the local fish buyers. During the long hours I spent at sea in Francie's company he talked about different methods of fishing and held the view that seine netting was the best. Even though seine netting was pie-in-the-sky as far as our boat was concerned, nevertheless it registered with me as something to be borne in mind for the future. A bigger and more powerful boat would certainly be required. Ever the optimist, I believed that somehow all things were possible.

Not one to stand still and wait for things to happen, and prompted by Francie's views on seining, James kept an eye on the 'boats for sale' columns of the *Fishing News* in the hope that something suitable might become available. Nothing happened immediately so they continued longlining with the *Tern*. It was far from ideal. For one thing, while the engine ran very well at speed, it constantly oiled up the plugs when running slow. Basically it meant that while fishing, James was fully occupied with changing plugs – something he became so adept at that he could do so without stopping the engine. Meanwhile, Francie had to work the long-lines on his own. It was hard work!

James recalls that the first glimmer of hope came when his father joined Francie and himself on the *Tern* for a spell during the summer. McLeod senior, whose predecessors had a fishing background, experienced first hand the difficulties encountered by the two men. It was during those long days at sea that James first mentioned his desire of getting a bigger boat to his father. By then, James did actually have details of suitable seining boats for sale in Scotland, but neither Tom Swan nor he had the ready cash to move on the venture. Mr McLeod senior was obviously impressed by what young James had to say, and out of the blue announced, 'Perhaps your mother and I can help.' While yet in its infancy, the McLeod dream had received an enormous boost, akin to Neil Armstrong's famous line, 'One small step for man, a giant leap for mankind.'

James and his father went across to Stranraer later that summer and checked out a few boats that were up for sale. One of them was the 40ft *Martha Helen*, which was fishing in Luce Bay at the southern side of the Stranraer peninsula. That was the boat they decided to buy. James's father, who took an instant liking to her, said, 'That's your boat.' McLeod senior would have preferred his son to be sole owner of the boat, but because of his association with Tom Swan, James felt obliged to offer him the option of having a share. With some difficulty Tom raised the money and the option was taken up.

As already mentioned, the *Martha Helen* was currently fishing and not immediately available. That suited James, who arranged to spend one month fishing on the vessel in Scotland before taking her over. He was, of course, he recalls, 'An unpaid crew member but it gave me an invaluable chance to learn something of the details of seine netting.' He explained:

> The seine netting referred to is also known as fly dragging. It is a method that evolved in Scotland and was based on Danish anchor seining, the difference being that an anchor is not used. Basically it is a bottom fishing method aimed mainly at catching demersal species such as haddock, whiting, cod and flat fish. Ropes of up to two miles in length are laid out from the boat as she moves to surround an area in an approximate triangular fashion. The net is shot at the point furthest from the boat. The two free ends of the warps are hauled in by a winch as the boat motors slowly ahead, herding fish inwards and into the path of the net. Fishing action is mainly due to the movement of the warps across the seabed, which disturbs and guides the fish within the area encircled.

The *Martha Helen* was handed over to James in November 1936. The plan was that the Scotch crew would accompany James to Belfast, where he would meet up with Francie for the remainder of the trip to Killybegs. As it so happened, the weather was atrocious that winter. Gale after gale meant that it took all of eight weeks to reach Killybegs. Over a month was spent weather-bound at Moville. James remembers, 'It was the first week in February 1937 when we arrived in Killybegs. The weather was so bad on the morning of our arrival that it took eight hours to make the normal two-hour passage from Rathlin O'Beirne into the harbour.'

Martha Helen.

In the months that followed history was made. The *Martha Helen*, skippered by James, was the first boat from which a seine net of the fly-dragging type was shot off the Killybegs coast. Indeed, the *Martha Helen* was the only local boat at that time capable of being used for that particular type of seining. It should, however, be mentioned that a local family, the Hegartys, had previously experimented to some extent with anchor seining. As James says:

> It took some time but gradually we began to do well seining. With Francie's extensive knowledge of fishing and my own seafaring acumen things began to look up. We got to know the grounds better! In September 1937 a tremendous spell of fishing began. Fish returned to the Bay. Haddock and whiting were plentiful and you were always sure of a few cod and some flats. It was great and, of course, we had no competition. Yet, all was not plain sailing.

James believed that fish buyers would be well disposed towards him when the boat was fishing on a regular basis and making good landings. On the contrary, he says, 'The fish buyers were initially not kindly towards us. If they got the fish for nothing, they wanted it for half nothing.' It was a situation that had to be faced up to if he and his crew were to make a decent living.

James McLeod, being James McLeod, was not going to sit back and do nothing. That was not his style; faint-hearted he was not! An alternative market for the fish had to be found. He explained how he went about it:

> The Irish Sea Fisheries Association were in existence at the time, so without informing our so-called local buyers I applied for membership of the Association. It had a superior marketing arrangement whereby your fish was taken at a list price and whatever they couldn't sell off locally was shipped to Dublin. I had to bide my time though because I wasn't an Irish citizen. That was sorted out in a few weeks, just at a time when our fishing was really improving … There is something that I always remind fishermen of, while the Irish Sea Fisheries Association came in for criticism, and may have been open to a measure of it, nevertheless it did have a decent structured arrangement when it came to buying fish from boats at that time. It gave a security and incentive that was not coming from any other quarter.

While Tom Swan didn't have a lot of spare cash when James offered him a share in the *Martha Helen*, that situation was to change when he married a wealthy lady. Tom was then in a position to propose buying another boat. James went to Scotland with him to look at two boats that were up for sale: one was a 45ft Fifie, the *Pursuit*, at St Monans, and the other was a 53ft Clyde-built herring ringer, the *Jeanette*. Tom preferred the ringer but James was uneasy about her because she had only 3ft 6in draught. When James expressed his preference for the Fifie, Tom said, 'In that case we'll take both.' That's what happened! All of a sudden James was involved with a fleet.

On my second visit to James, this time at his Killybegs home, he went on to recall various happenings during the 1940s and early '50s. He began by telling me that with the help of his brother he brought one of the boats purchased by Tom Swan in Scotland, the *Jeanette*, back to Killybegs. Francie McCallig, the man who had initially introduced James to fishing, was appointed skipper. When the second boat, the *Pursuit*, was ready for delivery, James again went to Scotland to fetch her. He arrived with her in the company of his father. But all was not well at the home port! James was informed that in his absence, Tom Swan, accompanied by his wife, had been to Killybegs and 'a whole rumpus' had arisen between the Swans and the crew the *Jeanette*. James's understanding up to that point was that he was to manage all the boats. That, apparently, was no longer the case. A now strained relationship meant the two parties would find it difficult to carry on a working relationship. James informed his father of the situation, who immediately advised him to buy out Tom Swan's share in the *Martha Helen*. That James did, and Tom was none too pleased. Subsequently Tom sacked the crew of the *Jeanette*, including Francie, and further distanced himself from the Killybegs scene and James by basing the boats *Jeanette* and *Pursuit* at Mullaghmore, County Sligo.

Pursuit. (Courtesy of Francis Cunningham)

From that point on they went their separate ways, with James as sole owner of the *Martha Helen*. James continued to fish out of Killybegs and as he recalls, 'We were doing very nicely, occasionally landing around seventy-five boxes per night.' With a glint in his eye he went on to say:

Of course we didn't inform the Swan boats about it. By then both vessels were crewed by men from the Mullaghmore/Ballyshannon area. Word that we were doing well quickly spread and it wasn't long until the Swan boats arrived out to fish beside us. That went on for a while but try as they might they couldn't match our landings. After a while the *Jeanette* began to land into Killybegs. She was the first Swan boat to do so since they transferred to Mullaghmore. On the *Jeanette* at that time, thought not as skipper, was a young chap named Albert Swan. Albert, who hailed from Dunmany, County Fermanagh, was a relative of my former working partner, Tom. Gradually he began to strike up conservations with me as I worked at gear on my boat or on the pier. Even though he never asked directly, I knew that Albert was trying to find out the reason why their catches were so poor in comparison to ours. Well, it has always been in my nature to help others and I had indeed been observing their fishing technique. When the subject was broached I explained to Albert that I believed the answer lay in the fact that they were hauling much too fast for the number of coils-aside they were using. As I saw it, they were trying to catch the fish before the fish got away from them, instead of actually fishing. My advice was acted upon with positive results. Albert was, of course, to later become a successful fisherman and a great businessman. For many years our families lived as friends and next-door neighbours at St Catherine's Road, Killybegs.

James was destined to have a hand in much of what went on in the development and progression of fishing at Killybegs. He financially helped Francie McCallig to get his own boat, the *Mary Buchan*, a fine Meevagh-built, 45ft vessel. He also fetched another boat from Scotland for a local owner. The fleet was further boosted when Albert Swan established himself and decided to base the *Jeanette* and the *Pursuit* at Killybegs in favour of Mullaghmore. Among the sceptics who predicted that the *Martha Helen* wouldn't last six months when she first arrived were those now interested

in getting boats. As James put it, 'We proved a point, Francie was right in his judgement and luckily I had been able to take advantage of it. In spite of original gloomy predictions by some pundits, people began to see the light.' He went on to say, 'Development was the natural course anyway; I was lucky in having been able to have a certain input. The boats would have come, probably in a different form and more slowly.'

As I sat listening to James, I couldn't believe my ears when he said, 'I went back to sea when the war started.' I asked what happened to the *Martha Helen*, 'Oh, she continued fishing with Tommy Cunningham as skipper.' I was still somewhat taken aback that this man, who up to then had been steeped in the development of the Killybegs fishing industry, decided to join the merchant navy. I was further surprised when he told me of his long-time yearning to join the RAF. Indeed, he would have done so had the recruiting officer not pointed out that persons holding second mate's tickets couldn't be considered for the RAF. Instead he went to sea. In a way that suited him better, because it afforded him the opportunity to serve the necessary time to acquire firstly his mate's ticket, and later his master's ticket. Throughout his life James maintained that he was incredibly fortunate; things always seem to fall into to place, 'I never tried to get into trouble nor did I particularly try to stay out of it, I just took things as they came.' His wartime experiences were exciting and indeed at times hair-raising, but those are stories for another day.

James married Glaswegian lass Anna after the war ended in 1945. They set up home in Killybegs. At the time, his intention was to return to sea when his leave period ended. However, he came down with malaria. Recovery took some time, at the end of which he decided to return to fishing at Killybegs. James's *Martha Helen* had continued to fish during the years he was at sea, and during his illness. Now, on principle, he wouldn't push a man out of the crew in order to make a berth for himself. Instead he took a berth on Francie's *Mary Buchan*, a boat that had done very well since her arrival. James was at great pains to point out that Francie had fully paid back all loans taken out in order to purchase the boat.

Now that things were ticking over nicely, James decided it was time to undertake a new challenge: he would have a new and bigger boat built. He explained as follows:

During the war, one of the advantages I had was that I never was a heavy spender, and, of course, the *Martha Helen* was making money all the time. Accordingly, I had enough money gathered to go to Jack Tyrell at Arklow in 1947 and order a new boat, a 50-footer; the size of boats had gradually increased. While I was waiting on the new boat, the *Mairead*, Tommy Cunningham, who skippered the *Martha Helen*, smashed his leg badly in an accident on the boat [he actually lost the leg, which was replaced by an artificial limb]. I transferred from the *Mary Buchan* to the replace Tommy. Again, things worked out well enough, because by the time the *Mairead* was ready, Tommy had sufficiently recovered from his leg injury to go back as skipper of the *Martha Helen*. In the meantime, the fleet had grown quickly. I have to say again that what Francie and I started had really blossomed more quickly than anyone could have expected.

As time went by, the engine in the *Martha Helen* began to give trouble and it was decided to have it replaced in Glasgow. On the way across, James says:

> The engine finally decided to give up the ghost. It could have chosen a better time and place than on the night of 30 January 1948 to do so! I remember the date because on that day Mahatma Ghandi, one-time political and spiritual of India, was assassinated. We were off Rathlin Island on the north Antrim coast when a storm unexpectedly blew up. Winds of up to 65mph were recorded in the area. We hoisted a mainsail and headed for Islay in the hope of getting into Loch Indaal, west of the Mull of Eo but didn't quite make it. An attempt at mooring failed, leaving the boat at the mercy of the storm. Eventually she went ashore and was badly damaged. Fortunately we all got off safely. That was the end of the *Martha Helen*.

During the late 1940s and early '50s James continued to very successfully fish the *Mairead*. I believe she was the first boat in Killybegs to have an echo sounder fitted. It was in the late 1940s that young Killybegs teenager Tommy Watson joined the crew of the *Mairead*. Tommy was later to become legendry in fishing circles in Killybegs and beyond. James, his great mentor, described him as, 'An outstanding fisherman, truly brilliant.'

Left to right: Casamara, Moravia, Kincora, Kittiwake.

Around 1954, James decided the time had come to have a bigger boat built. Back he went to Jack Tyrrell and this time ordered a 60ft boat. On delivery of James's new boat, the *Muiranna*, Tommy Watson, then a mere twenty years old, and another chap bought the *Mairead* from James.

Now it was as if the floodgates began to open as far as boats on the Irish coast were concerned. James recalls that:

> H.J. Nolan (Dublin), had a big input to Irish fishing. First of all, in the late 1940s, they were responsible for bringing the four Thomson brothers and their superb boats, the *Casamara, Moravia, Kittiwake,* and *Kincora,* over from Scotland. The brothers were extremely experienced fishermen who gave a very big lift to seine net fishing. Nolan's also brought over a pair of Scottish herring ringers at a time when interest in herring fishing had began to grow.

It was also a time when a number of boats arrived in Killybegs, including Albert Swan's *Evening Star* and the *Siobhan*, belonging to Willie McCallig, who had previously fished on one of the 'Nolan boats'. In the years that followed boats came thick and fast. Amongst those to purchase new vessels were Willie's brothers George and Johnny, and the Moore brothers Martin, Mossy, Benny and Paddy.

James McLeod keeping a watchful eye on proceedings from the *Muiranna*'s wheelhouse, 1967. (Courtesy of the *Marine Times*)

Aboard the *Muiranna, c.*1959 are, from left to right, back row: Brian Ellis, Brian Kelly, Seamus McGuinness, Noel Kyles, and an unknown Swedish fisherman. Front row: James McLeod, John Rodden and Seamus Tully. (Courtesy of Francis Cunningham)

As James further reflected on the development of fishing in the Killybegs area he spoke glowingly of the 'Kerry boats' owned by the Moore family who came to Donegal in the 1930s. He recalls:

They were trawling behind St John's Point even before we got the *Martha Helen*. One family member, Martin, moved to live at Killybegs in the 1930s. Martin was a particularly intelligent man and when he saw us seine netting he was determined to get into it. To that end he purchased a boat called the *Mulroy Bay* that was lying up in Meevagh and had her re-engined. He was fortunate that his father, who fished with him, looked after the engine, and indeed you could have taken your breakfast off the floor of the engine room, so clean and tidy was it.

Willie McCallig's *Siobhan* and James McLeod's *Muiranna* were similar boats; in fact virtually sister ships. In the early years both were successful seine netters. However, with the demand for herring increasing, it was desirable that they should also get involved in that particular winter fishing. Unfortunately, as James says, 'The boats were unsuitable for herring ringing which was almost exclusively the method used at the time. The designs were completely wrong. Basically they were intended for seine netting.' So what was to be done? Was there any other form of herring fishing which would lend itself to the boats in question? In 1956, Willie and James discussed the situation and a decision was taken that James should go to Scandinavia in order to investigate what options might be available. James recalls that, 'BIM (An Bord Iascaigh Mhara) was very helpful in that it lined up contacts for him, and in return he submitted a report to the Bord on the survey he carried out.'

He surveyed various herring-fishing methods at several ports. In Norway, larger boats in the 30-40m length category carried out purse seining (herring ringing) with the seine being operated by two dories. Technological developments were soon to dramatically change the methodology of fishing, with the two-dory seiners being completely phased out by the late 1960s. There was also a smaller net, a Dekk-Snurper, which could be operated by one boat. That, James says:

> …was a single-boat herring purse seine. It had possibilities where we were concerned and we did give it serious consideration. Meanwhile Gundry of Bridport made a similar net that was tried by the Cornish boat *Sweet Promise*. When I spoke to her skipper at Dunmore East he told me that the net had not been altogether successful in our waters. Consequently Willie and I decided not to pursue that method.

A further approach that James had come across in Denmark during his Scandinavian survey was pair-fishing using a pelagic (mid-water) trawl. While there he went fishing on a couple of Swedish boats. That gave him the opportunity to study the practicalities and to generally familiarise himself with handling the gear. He satisfied himself that the two boats *Muiranna* and *Siobhan* could successfully operate the pelagic trawl for herring fishing. Willie, who was paying half the expenses involved in the survey, agreed, and the two men set about adapting the hauling machinery on their boats. That involved the removal of existing winches, coilers and fittings in order to make way for the new Danish trawl winches. Another detail recalled by James was that he and Willie erred on the side of caution by choosing combination winches; winches which could be used for seining or the pelagic trawling. In his quiet but deliberate manner he went on to say:

> Subsequently as other skippers became interested in the pelagic trawl, as they soon did, I advised them to get the pure trawling winch as the combination variety was not 100 per cent effective. You learn from your mistakes, but I always tried to help by telling people as honestly as I could what I had discovered from my own experiences.

With the winches fitted at the local boatyard and the pelagic trawls on board, the *Muiranna* and *Siobhan* headed for sea under the guidance of their respective skippers. First attempts at fishing were largely exploratory and very much part of a learning curve. Day fishing wasn't going well at all, so it was decided to try night fishing. James recalls:

> We went up the west coast but didn't catch anything of any consequence. We came back down and persevered locally for some considerable time. It wasn't until one night off the waterfall on the south side of Ros Beg Bay that we had our first real success; we got seventy cran of herring. We carried on for the season and despite considerable teething problems our landings were fully on a par with the 'ringers'. That the pelagic trawl was particularly well suited to conditions on this coast became clear. Indeed, there were occasions when the bulk of herring caught was so great that fish died and sunk the net. It was not unknown for skippers of 'ringers' who happened to be close by looking for markings to come and help us get our net hauled by putting some of their crew members aboard our boats.
>
> The fact that we could catch fish in large quantities soon became apparent to everybody. We were on the right track but needed to improve our handling methods, especially the boarding of heavy bags of fish. As with

most problems, through time a solution was found. The boat's rigging was changed to incorporate two derricks, one on the foremast in addition to the regular aft derrick. That arrangement facilitated a lifting and splitting system, allowing the bag to be raised and emptied in stages. Within two years the whole fleet was changing over to pelagic trawls and for the most part 'ring netting' became a thing of the past. A major plus was that the pelagic trawl (often referred to as a mid-water trawl) fished from the seabed to the surface, whereas the 'ring net' really needed fish to be near the surface and preferably in fairly sheltered conditions.

As is the case in most facets of life, nothing stands still for long. The improved method of catching herring meant that larger quantities were being caught. That, in turn, suggested that bigger boats would be a more lucrative proposition for fishermen. James and his near neighbour Albert Swan discussed the situation. James, pointing to the garden wall at his home, says:

> I well remember Albert and I stood out there and talked about the next move. Albert at first wasn't sure about what to do, but having sourced as much relevant information as he could both at home and abroad, he decided on a bigger boat. That decision resulted in Albert having the 80ft *Mallrin* built in 1967. The following year Tommy Watson did likewise and went for a similar boat, the *Sanpaulin*.

According to James, 'They made the correct decision'. So it would seem: the move proved an enormous success for the two men who had already made names for themselves on the pelagic scene, initially fishing Alberts' *Christine* with Tommy's *Easter Morn*. Tommy later exchanged the *Easter Morn* for the *Radiance* before acquiring the *Sanpaulin*. James continued:

> I made a mistake; Willie and I re-engined our boats instead of going for larger vessels. But I had other considerations at the time that caused me to hesitate, not least that my family, a boy and three girls were at a critical stage in their schooling. However, we live with what we do! It certainly would have been better if I had moved up; Albert made the right move, and as I already said elsewhere Tommy Watson was an absolutely brilliant fisherman and boat handler.

James also mentioned that by the early 1960s, Albert was a BIM board member. That enabled Albert to have suggestions implemented that were first recommended by James in a report submitted by him to BIM. The report was based James's fact-finding trip to the Scandinavian countries. Principal among the suggestions was having a knowledgeable man or two sent over from Sweden to help out with fishing gear problems in Ireland. One such problem that had long baffled fishermen was how best to keep the headline of the trawl up when it was being towed. Floats, which at first seemed the obvious solution, were later deemed to flatten out horizontally when being towed through the water and if anything had an adverse effect because they tended to sink and thereby take the headline down.

When a Swedish gentleman did eventually come to Ireland, he was, James says:

> …kindly sent to Dunmore East by BIM to examine a new unused net that
> I had aboard my boat. As a result, the solution to the problem of keeping the
> headline up was solved by stretching and tensioning the net at the headline
> to the extent that when towed the water billowed the net in a similar fash-
> ion to wind billowing a sail.

While James was still fishing, he became associated with the fishing-net-making firm of Bridport-Gundry Ltd. The association came about through contact with a gentleman called Hugh Norman. Hugh had previously worked with Gourock Ropeworks Co. Ltd, Scotland, a firm that had advanced into net-making. It was when James had problems with knots slipping in the meshes of nets, resulting in bags exploding when under pressure from large volumes of fish, that he first met Hugh in the mid-1960s. The suggestion that James should link up with Gundry's was spurred on by two factors: firstly, Gundry's feared they were losing touch with fishing in Ireland and needed a base here, and secondly, because James was having a large shed built. The shed was to be used as an indoor facility for working at fishing gear. Along came Hugh before the building was completed and effectively invited James into partnership with Bridport-Gundry Ltd. The bones of the proposition made were that, when completed, the building would be handed over to Gundry's, who would establish a net-making factory therein, and that James, as a board member, would serve in an advisory capacity while still fishing; on retirement he would be employed in a full-time managerial capacity. As a result of discussing the matter with his wife and taking into account that their family was not interested in fishing, the decision was taken to accept the Gundry proposal. On retirement James, who was not interested in becoming overall manager of the business, took an active part in the technical side of net-making. The company, which was to earn a solid reputation at home and abroad, became extremely successful.

In 1974, Albert Swan set up another net-making firm, Swan Net Ltd, at Killybegs. Through Albert's considerable business acumen and expertise Swan Net Ltd expanded rapidly and gained a prestigious place in the world of net-making. In 2000, as a result of Swan Net's international acclaim, the Hampidjan group, a powerful Iceland-based concern with interests throughout the world, acquired a shareholding in the Killybegs-based company. In 2002, Gundry's Ltd and Swan Net Ltd amalgamated within the Hampidjan Group to form Swan Net-Gundry Ltd.

I asked James about leisure activities he was involved in over the years. I was to learn that flying and sailing were the most favoured. As to flying he says:

I was always keen on flying and it stemmed back to a very young age, possibly around three years. Just across the railways line from where I grew up at Montrose, Scotland, there was a golf course, and alongside it was an aerodrome at which number-two squadron of the old Royal Flying Corps was established. It served as a training unit. I can remember standing beside the airfield with more senior family members watching planes flying. That was probably when my interest in aircraft and flying started to develop.

Several years passed before he actually took to the air. This is how he recalls it:

My inaugural flight in an aircraft was in Australia during the first year of my apprenticeship in a merchant ship. I squandered the immense sum of 10s when my total monthly wage was 20s or £1. In 1932, when jobs at sea became scarce and I was unemployed, I joined a flying club in Scotland.

As I have often put it, I had saved hard for the six months when I was at sea and then went bust in a fortnight. It was worth it, I got my PPL (A) licence, which meant I had flown solo. I didn't get the opportunity to fly for along time after that.

James continued:

It was in later life when family responsibilities began to wane that I took up flying again. On that occasion my daughter Jillian advised me to get on with it, and stop talking about it. So I did! Mind you, I had to go back to square one because my PPL (A) licence had not been kept up to date. I should mention that my late wife Anna, who had an inherent fear of being off the ground, didn't at any time discourage me from pursuing my hobby. Off I went and took some more lessons at Newtownards, County Down, and St Angelo, County Fermanagh, thereby repossessing my PPL (A). Sometime later a few friends, flying acquaintances and myself decided to club together and buy an aircraft. It was to be just for pleasure purposes. As time went by some of the prospective buyers backed out, however, two friends and I went ahead with the venture. It was very nice to have the aircraft there and you could go down and fly it as you pleased.

When I asked James about any hair-raising or memorable incidents during his long career at sea, I was expecting that he might mention getting off the stricken *Martha Helen* near the rugged Islay coastline on that stormy winter's night. However, it was another incident involving the *Martha Helen* that he told me about, 'Johnny McCloskey and myself were just splitting a bag of fish when she took a lurch and shot me out over the side. It was a beautiful swallow dive that left me about 20ft from the boat.' Jokingly, he went on to say:

When relating the story I point out that the crew were hopping around in a semi-panic while I was the coolest man there, but then, of course, I was water-cooled. The fact is I wasn't too worried because I was on the lee-side of the boat which was drifting towards me. I told the crew what to do. Temporarily there was air trapped in my oilskin so I was quite buoyant.

I could have kicked off my boots but decided not to. I was used to swimming and hadn't swallowed any water. When the boat drifted over the crew put a lifebuoy over the side and helped me back on board none the worse for my experience.

He did also refer to one or two close shaves during his war years on merchant ships. Thankfully he and the crews came through unscathed.

As we stood talking prior to my departure from this remarkable gentleman's home at St Catherine's Road, Killybegs, he referred me to some family photographs that adorned the sitting room sideboard and walls. Firstly he pointed to the several images of his lovely wife, Anna, who sadly succumbed to a prolonged illness in 1983. Satisfaction, in the sense of a job well done, rather than pride was what showed on the man's face as pointed out his son and daughters. Perhaps, though, it was the cheerful faces of the even younger generation that went closest to bringing on a smile.

Long after I left the his home, and indeed up to the present time, which is now several months later, I can't help wondering if my writings can ever do justice to the vocational achievements, determination and commitment of James McLeod. This man is certainly a one-off! That he left no stone unturned to further the cause of fishing at Killybegs is, I believe, an undisputed fact. He saw problems as being there to be solved, not tolerated. He went forth, discovered and spread the fishing gospel in a way that few people in the 1930s and '40s would have dreamed of. It happened in an age when travel abroad and international communication were not taken for granted as they are today. The fact that funds were not always as plentiful as they might have been did not deter him. Not only did Killybegs benefit from the pioneering attributes of this generous man, but so did the fishing fraternity at other ports around the coast.

It may be that young men of today regard it all as old hat and irrelevant. Certainly modern techniques, equipment and gadgetry introduced as fishing aids in more recent times have made much of the work done by James and his contemporaries obsolete. Yet it should be remembered that initiatives introduced in those days were vital stepping stones where the future of Irish fishing was concerned. The lengths he went to to further the fishing cause should not be forgotten.

James is now in his ninety-seventh year. His input to various facets of the fishing industry would alone place him as man apart. Perhaps, though, it was the occasional changes in lifestyle and the activities he became involved with that really set him apart. Let us remember that during the war he left his boat to be fished by others while he signed up to a merchant shipping company. Then there were the flirtations with flying, which culminated with him becoming part owner of a plane. Sailing is also included in his repertoire of achievements. Indeed, his name is inscribed no fewer than six times as winner on the Killybegs Cruisers Regatta Cup in the 1930s and '40s. He is by no means a man of half measures.

IMPORTANCE OF A GOOD CREW

TOM FERGUSON OF SKERRIES, COUNTY DUBLIN

The world is well endowed with singular individuals but I believe there is a category made up of some who are more singular that others. Almost from the moment I sat down to converse with Tom Ferguson the sense that I was indeed in the company of one from the latter group was ever present. Unassuming, pleasant, soft-spoken and genial are just a few of the adjectives one might use when describing the now-retired Skerries fisherman.

Because of health reasons, Tom was forced to withdraw from what had been a distinguished career as a high-profile man of the seas at the age of fifty-seven. It was a career that began at the age of fourteen when, after leaving national school, he joined the crew of his father's boat, the *Ros Cathail* (D125). He acquired a skipper's ticket at the age of twenty-one and by the time of his retirement in 1999 he had become the owner of no fewer than four newly built vessels. His first boat, the 56ft *Ard Gillen* (D453) joined the Skerries fleet in 1967. By the time he sailed away from Baltimore seventeen years later with the brand new 120ft 'tank boat' *Sean-Pol* (D641), he had put two further boats through his hands.

That young Tom took up fishing as a career was unlikely to have caused surprise in Skerries. He was merely following a well-established family tradition. Fishing had been an ancestral way of life for the Ferguson clan since their arrival from Scotland at the port of Loughshinney in the 1800s. In 1825, they first ventured forth in an 18ft yawl to harvest the nearby east-coast fishing grounds.

At the age of twenty-four Tom became Skerries' youngest boat owner when he purchased the Killybegs-built *Ard Gillen*. This bold move, which involved a BIM hire-purchase agreement on the £24,000 cost of the boat, was a clear demonstration of the initiative, ambition, and acumen of this young man. Four years later, Tom took another enormous stride forward when the *Ard Gillen* passed on to his brother Michael and he took delivery of the then state-of-the-art *Kenure* (D359), a 70ft vessel costing over £74,000. An indication of how deeply fishing was ingrained in the Ferguson family is that while Tom was busy procuring the *Kenure*, his brother Terence was having the 52ft *Wild Wave* built at Crosshaven. A further boat in the ownership of the Ferguson family around that time was the *Golden Fleece*. Yet another brother, Peter, was poised to become a crew member of the *Kenure*. By 1975 the Ferguson family had a fleet of modern boats based at Skerries. At the launch of the *Kenure* at Killybegs in 1971, the BIM Secretary of the day, Seosamh MacArtain, stated:

> It is particularly appropriate that this first 70ft vessel should be built for one of the leading skippers from the Skerries/Loughshinney area or indeed the whole coast. We could not wish for a better man to initiate fishing this new vessel design and we can wish you every success with the utmost confidence.

Obviously, Tom's ventures into bigger, better and more modern boats were paying dividends, because in 1977 he had the 86ft *Shenick* built at Fraserburgh, Scotland. During the launching ceremony of the Dublin-registered stern trawler on Friday 14 October 1977, at the Sandhaven boatyard of J. & G. Forbes, Fr Alister Doyle, Peterhead, blessed the vessel. The blessing was reported in the *Fraserburgh Herald* as follows, 'It is believed to be the first of its kind ever held in the Buchan area.' Unusual also was the flying of the tricolour. Apparently the ceremony attracted many onlookers who seemed to enjoy the occasion.

Tom Ferguson, 2009.

Had all the dreams and ambitions of the Loughshinney-born man been fulfilled, or were there still opportunities to be seized upon? Well the answers are, no to the first part, and yes to the second. Proof comes in the form of a 120ft 'tank boat'. Yes, at the age of forty-one Tom really moved into the big time when, in 1984, he took delivery of his new £2.1 million vessel, *Sean-Pol*. By then it was clear for all to see that he was an extremely successful fisherman.

So it was to continue until fate determined otherwise. In 1998/99 he suffered a stroke that would rule him out of taking part in any further fishing activities.

People sometimes wonder how the names of particular boats are determined. In the case of Tom's vessels it was links with the local area that inspired the names of the first three, while *Sean-Pol* is the combined names of his sons John and Paul. The *Ard Gillen* was named after a well-known nearby castle of the same name. The Kenure Estate in the Loughshinney/

Ard Gillen at Arklow, 2007.

Rush area prompted the name *Kenure*, while Shenick is the largest of three low-lying islands just off the coast at Skerries. The east-to-west sloping island with its Martello tower is in full view from the sitting room of the Ferguson home, The Mews, Holmpatrick. I'm told the island can be reached on foot from the shore at low water.

Most of what I have written to date is factual and could indeed be derived from archives. But what of the man with whom I spent the afternoon chatting? The most striking thing about him was the almost complete absence of negativity in any aspect of his life. It seemed as if his fishing career had been one long, enjoyable experience. There were none of the usual complaints about poor fish prices or being badly treated by one organisation or another. During our entire conversation he spoke of how good things had been. 'All my boats were lucky boats,' he said. He spoke highly of the people he rubbed shoulders with over the years. Among those were Castletownbere men Kieran O'Driscoll, Larry Murphy and Mick Orpen, each of whom he 'paired fished' with at different times. He recalled that Kieran's boat was named *Spes Nova* and that Larry Murphy fished a boat called the *Fiona Patricia*. Other names from those days that came to mind were Joe Joe O'Sullivan and the late Frank Downey. He spoke also of the O'Driscoll brothers, Donal and the late Billy, who he described as 'nice men and great fishermen'.

He smiled as he reflected on one particular occasion when the *Kenure* 'paired' with Larry Murphy's *Fiona Patricia* in Dunmore East. The story goes as follows:

> Fishing had been slack for awhile. There was little doing to the east so Larry and I thought we would go west along and try a shot off Ballycotton. Well, so plentiful were the herring that we loaded down the two boats in as many shots. We headed back and tied up at Dunmore East where we were told that fishing had been very poor with the other boats. The upshot was that we got top price for our two boat loads of fish. We were so please that we were literally jumping with joy! When over the phone, Dolores, my wife, asked me to help choose a name for our new baby daughter, I had no hesitation in proposing Fiona, after Larry's boat with which we landed the lucrative catch. The baby was indeed christened Fiona.

Tom also talked about the importance of a good crew. The numbers of crew members varied from boat to boat over the years, but in as far a possible he regarded the men as associates rather than employees. Yet, the men knew where they stood. They were not permitted to drink alcohol on the job and even on freezing winter's nights they had to be on deck ready to react whenever fish showed, 'I may have wanted them to do this or that at the drop of a hat; there would be no time to go looking for them. When the fish showed up on the sounder it was all go.' Tom pondered further on crew members:

> They needed to be fit, with no ailments, and they needed to have respect for one another. One antisocial person or troublemaker could cause lots of problems in a crew. Understandably, one of the most monotonous and disliked jobs carried out by crew members was 'tailing' prawns. I had great crews over the years. There were always ten or eleven on the *Sean-Pol*.

In his role as skipper, once he took charge of his own boat it was a case of being on his toes all the time. He explained the reasons for this:

> As well as being at the wheel and keeping an eye on deck activities, you were constantly checking the instrument panel. At times during herring fishing in Dunmore East there were as many as seventy boats moving around within a square mile. There were lights coming at you from all directions! The whole time you had to watch out for your gear and wires, as well as keeping an eye on the closeness of the shore, rocks and other boats.

While Tom engaged in all kinds of fishing, he believes that herring were the Irish fisherman's bonanza in the 1970s. He went on to say:

Shenick at Frazerburg, 1977.

If the fish were present at all, they were plentiful, and you could fill the hold with them. They were easy to deal with; no gutting or other preparation before sale like you had with other kinds of fish. Yet, getting started at the herring was an expensive business and you were taking a chance. You had to have at least three or four nets costing in the region of £2,000 each. A lot of money in the 1970s! It is true that Dunmore East herring fishing could either make or break a fisherman. If the herring didn't run, all the work and expense was for nothing. The fact that herring go for shoal water near rocks didn't help, because if you went too close and tore your net the consequences were dire in terms of both time and money. Fortunately for me, we were lucky, Dunmore East fishing was very good to us.

That the young Skerries man of the 1960s travelled far along the road to success since the day he took delivery of the *Ard Gillen* is no secret. He admits that he made a very good living as a fisherman. Perhaps the pinnacle of his ambition was reached with the coming of the *Sean-Pol*. 'It was a lovely boat,' he says. Indeed, it was, and a far cry from the *Ard Gillen*! Part of the make-up included tanks capable of holding up to 180 tonnes of fish, an array of computerised instrumentation, eleven bunks and a carpeted skipper's cabin, the decor of which was overseen by Tom's wife, Dolores. Even allowing for the fact that government grants and FEOGA helped with the cost, Tom's monetary input was still substantial. Nevertheless, he obviously believed that there was a future in fishing at the time. Fishing, he said:

> …was not only a way of making money but also a great adventure in life. I would do it all over again without hesitation if things were the same. Unfortunately everything has changed. Nowadays quotas, bureaucracy, accountability and umpteen other obstacles have been put in place to stop you fishing. Now I wouldn't even consider setting out on a fishing career. Thankfully my sons did not follow the family tradition.

Tom also spoke of his father, Terence (Teddy), the man initially responsible for encouraging him to pursue a fishing career. Sadly, in October 1975, at the age of sixty-three, Teddy collapsed and died at the wheel of the

Sean-Pol (renamed *Myrebuen I*). (Courtesy of Tor-Erik, Harstad, Norway)

Ard Gillan. The boat was then owned by his son Michael. He was one of the best-known fishermen on the east coast and had been chairman of the Skerries and Loughshinney Fishermen's Association for many years. During that time he saw Skerries grow in stature as a fishing port. He must have been extremely proud of the way in which his family had contributed to that particular growth.

Perhaps retirement came a little earlier than Tom would have chosen. Nevertheless he now lives a life of luxury, with Dolores pandering to his every wish.

It was late afternoon when I bade Tom goodbye. Coolness had crept into the air by then. I believe he would have been out for his daily trip along the Skerries seafront earlier if I hadn't delayed him. Even so he would still go. Dolores assured me that come rain, hail, wind or sunshine, he headed off every day. My visit to the Ferguson home had indeed been a great pleasure.

IF ONLY IT WAS LOOKED AFTER

TEDDY O'SHEA OF KILLYBEGS, COUNTY DONEGAL

Teddy O'Shea, who originally hailed from Castletownbere, County Cork, has long been resident at Killybegs, County Donegal. Most southern fishermen who moved to the Donegal port made their way directly via the west coast. Not so with Teddy, he initially fished out of Howth. That's because shortly after finishing at national school, an institution of which he hasn't fond memories, he joined his brother Gerry, who had earlier abandoned the south in favour of east coast lure. As a fifteen-year-old he began fishing in Gerry's boat, the *Primula*. On the crew at the time was a young man called Mick Doyle from Redcross, County Wicklow. He had no fishing background and just came looking for a job. Gerry took him on! Later, another teenager joined the crew. He too was a virtually unknown young man, who hailed from Achill Island, County Mayo; a chap who began his fisherman's apprenticeship on Willie Reynolds' *Eiscir Riada* (D361) at Balbriggan. That young man was Kevin McHugh. What an impact the trio were to make on the Irish fishing industry in subsequent years!

Their journey began in the early 1960s, when Teddy, along with Mick Doyle, successfully completed the 'skipper course' at Galway. At the time Gerry O'Shea owned a number of boats, one of which was the

43

Teddy O'Shea taking it easy at his Killybegs home.

St Bernadette (D57). She was for sale at Howth but there were no takers. When Teddy had achieved skipper status, Gerry suggested that he should fish the *St Bernadette* rather than having her lying idle. So he did, out of Howth for some time, but he moved away from the east coast to Killybegs fairly quickly. Mick Doyle, Kevin McHugh and Teddy's sixteen-year-old brother Pierce went along with him. Teddy, who was then around twenty-two years of age, recalls that, 'There was plenty of fish to be caught.' All went well from the beginning and soon Teddy purchased his own boat, the *Charlotte Chambers*, from the Castletownbere partnership of Frank Downey and Joe Joe O'Sullivan. She was, he says, 'a bit rough but she made money for everyone who owned her'. Things began to move fairly quickly. It was a case of upwards and onwards. In 1968, Teddy took delivery of the brand new 75ft Norwegian-built *Sheanne*. Mick Doyle did likewise by taking delivery of a similar boat, the *Avril Marie*.

In the years that immediately followed, the *Sheanne* and *Avril Marie*, under the guiding hands of their respective owners, became a formidable duo, with winter herring fishing at Dunmore East and working out of Killybegs during the summer months. Fortune favours the brave, and so it was with Teddy, who went on to acquire a series of bigger and better boats, culminating with the present *Sheanne*, a 200ft tank boat with a carrying capacity of 1,200 tons. She was built in 2003. In between came no fewer that four other vessels. First it was the *John Karen*, next it was the second *Sheanne*. She was followed by the third *Sheanne*. Along the way, a fourth boat, a beamer, the *Grove* was also owned by Teddy. The second and third *Sheanne's* were tank boats; the *John Karen* was not originally. However she did have tanks fitted at a later date.

What came across as I listened to what Teddy had to say about the years following his arrival at Killybegs, was the camaraderie that existed between himself, Mick Doyle and Kevin McHugh. Certainly their fishing activities seemed significantly entwined. The obvious amity that existed led to immense success. He recalled the lucrative years of pairing at Dunmore East and working off Tory Island during summer months. What some describe as the 'golden era' of Irish fishing was about to take off. Teddy recalls:

The *St Bernadette* at Castletownbere pier, 1957.

Young men of yesteryear celebrate! Teddy and Kevin McHugh at Killybegs, late 1970s. (Courtesy of the *Irish Skipper*)

There was plenty of fish around then. We were into the mackerel at that stage. There were loads of them! There were also very good years of herring when the North Sea closed. Prices went away up; we were getting over £20 a box then. Mackerel were also plentiful; you could scarcely catch the herring because of them. Herring were in close to the shore but whenever you went off the slightest bit you got a bag full of mackerel. The market for large landings of mackerel was very poor at that time. It was only when the tank boats arrived that we began to develop a market with the 'old eastern block' countries. I put tanks in the *John Karen* but it wasn't a great success; she was just not suitable. Then I got the second *Sheanne,* she was, of course, a purpose-built tank boat.

Teddy regards fishing in the late 1970s and '80s as virtually the ultimate one can aspire to. There was, he says, 'no quotas until 1983. It was a case of going out, filling up and coming back in. There was no bother.' He smiled as he recalled an occasion when mackerel fishing north of the Minches, off the west coast of Scotland:

It was in the early 1980s. Based at Killybegs at that time was Ireland's most modern fleet of super-trawlers. Included were *Antarctic* (Kevin

McHugh), *Western Viking* (Seamus Tully), *Paula* (Mick Doyle), *Atlantean* (Des Faherty) and Teddy's *Sheanne*.

> Six of us set out from Killybegs. We headed for the Minches, channels that separate the Outer Hebrides from the Inner Hebrides and mainland Scotland. Seas were running very high when markings showed up at ninety fathoms. It was one of the biggest markings I have ever seen. Working together the six boats filled each other up, passing the bags of fish to the nearest vessel with tank space left. All the fish were taken in only nine tows, that's an average of over 350 tons per shot. We returned to Killybegs the following day after a remarkable trip and landed a total of 3,200 tons of mackerel. In a port where large landings were not then uncommon that particular one certainly did cause quite a stir.

'Ah, but those were the good old days,' says Teddy. Gradually mismanagement and draconian measures meted out by bureaucrats at home and abroad have ensured that sea-going where Irish fishermen are concerned is all but forbidden. As a consequence the industry in this country is on the brink of extinction.

All fishermen I meet with are disillusioned, concerned and saddened by what they see as a virtual abandonment of the industry by successive governments of this country. Many are convinced that the ultimate aim of our rulers is to reduce fishing effort to a point where an industry will no longer exist. Fish will, of course, continue to be imported and processors will continue to function, but fishermen will become a thing of the past. That is what fishermen believe. Individual grievances are naturally seen from the viewpoint of whichever sector a person is operating in. Not surprisingly, Teddy's concerns are pelagic based. He regards EU sanctioned quotas granted to the men on this island, when compared to the percentage of TAC (Total Allowable Catch) granted to the other countries, as ridiculous and unfair. He points to blue whiting as an example:

> We started fishing blue whiting years ago. Then the EU stopped us! Why? Because, we were told, the tonnage being caught was too great. Yet the Icelanders and the Faeroese were allowed to fish on. In fact they were given

a bigger quota while we got nothing. To keep within the confines of the TAC someone had to lose out and, of course, it was us. What they are doing is crazy! I sold my third *Sheanne* to a Faeroese company who with that one boat alone were allowed to catch more blue whiting than all the boats in Killybegs put together. The quota here is now so little that it's hardly worth going out. We didn't even bother last year.

He went on to say:

I was in Spain recently where blue whiting and scads were fetching higher prices than mackerel. We should have been allowed to fish blue whiting here. The Norwegians, who are not in the EU, fish down here and actually land at Killybegs. The whole thing is completely out of control.

Teddy is also dissatisfied with the restrictions placed on boat owners engaged in mackerel fishing. Our boats, he says, 'fish a couple of months at the beginning of the year and are tied up for the remainder'. He continued:

In the last few years huge shoals of mackerel have turned up, following a couple of very big years of breeding mackerel were caught at Rockall, a place they never were before. So plentiful were the fish that while boarding catches the excessive weight caused boats to lose brailers. The *Sheanne* caught 700 tons in one shot lasting three minutes.

When I asked how massive boats that are tied up for ten months of each year can be a feasible proposition, the reply came, 'Those boats are not too expensive to run. Money from other business interests was invested in the *Sheanne*. That left repayments low.'

On the question of herring fishing, Teddy disagrees with the scientists who say that stocks are low. On the contrary, he believes that stocks are high, 'Along the south coast they reckon you could nearly walk on them and off the Donegal coast it's only a matter of going out and catching all you want.' He is now of the opinion that herring spawn both in October and January, and not just October as previously thought. A different lot, no doubt, but certainly fish caught in January are spawning at that time.

So where has it all gone so badly wrong? Well, there isn't a fisherman that I know who does not lay the blame at the doors of the EU, and to a marginally lesser extent on our own government. Occasionally government ministers and negotiators get off the hook on the basis of being naive or browbeaten when it comes to dealing with experienced and manipulative EU bureaucrats. Teddy is of the opinion that Irish fishermen and the industry they represent is looked upon most unfavourably at the very highest level within the European Commission.

Coming in for criticism at home is the multi-body government approach to the industry. Teddy believes that a unified and centralised approach would be more effective. As it is, the Department of Agriculture, Fisheries and Food, An Bord Iascaigh Mhara, and the Marine Institute are all involved. Admin is, he says, 'spread all over the place. There are fisheries officers and civil servants scattered in their hundreds from Clonakilty to Cavan most of whom seem intent on making life as difficult as possible for the Irish fisherman.' He believes the country 'is too political, with the jobs for the boys scenario always lurking'. He also laments the fact that what could have been an everlasting industry in this country has been frittered away. If only, he says:

> …it was looked after. Mackerel fishing and processing alone could have been a massive business. There was a time when Killybegs fishing accounted for more treasury tax than the town of Letterkenny. Killybegs was the top earnings town in Donegal. Sadly, though, whatever money they collected from us was wasted. Mismanagement was terrible.

Reflecting back to his early days fishing out of Howth, Teddy recalls that mesh size mattered little to most fishermen working at the port. Nobody seemed to care as a long as boat loads of fish were landed. Serious damage was done to inshore stocks by catching very large quantities of undersized fish over a prolonged period. His brother Gerry, who always used a standard mesh, landed only mature fish. In addition to conserving stocks he also got better prices. Few followed his example and there was not an enforcer in sight.

I asked Teddy if such a successful fisherman had any particular memories of his days at sea. The only thing he could recall was having his shaving badly interrupted one morning on the *Charlotte Chambers*, while on passage down the river from Waterford:

> I was shaving and the next thing I heard was the sound of the boat going astern. I looked up to see that a collision had taken place between a coaster and our boat. The coaster actually went ashore after hitting us. Our boat was right up against the shore on the other side. We hit a few rocks but no serious damage was done.

He also recalled that his brother Gerry once said to him, 'I can't understand how you turned out to be such a good fisherman because you were a useless deckhand.' Obviously he has a great affinity with Gerry, whose name he mentioned several times. He smiled as he recalled another remark made by Gerry to a reluctant crew member, 'There is only room for one lazy so-and-so on this boat and that's me.'

I enjoyed taking with Teddy, now fifteen years retired from seagoing. With business interests and travel now prominent in his life he is seldom at a loose end. However, that afternoon, in the relaxed atmosphere of his home, we had wonderfully informal chat.

I LOVED MY JOB

DONAL O'DRISCOLL OF CASTLETOWNBERE, COUNTY CORK

It was in early June that I visited Donal O'Driscoll at Castletownbere. He was recovering from a hip operation but, as on previous occasions, I was warmly welcomed by himself and Maisie at their West End home. I spent a whole afternoon in the company of the man who has devoted a lifetime to the fishing industry, not only at sea, but also ashore, where he has tirelessly represented fishermen's causes at all levels. While our conversation that day concentrated mainly on Donal's fishing-related career, we did occasionally reminisce on our younger days in Baltimore and on Sherkin Island, the locations we grew up in during the 'good old days' of the 1940s and early 1950s. As a child, along with Hannah, a lady who helped my mother, I well remember looking forward to visiting the O'Driscoll family home on Sherkin Island. Little did I know then that long past half a century later, I would be sitting with Donal at his adopted Castletownbere discussing his lifetime.

While still of school-going age on Sherkin Island, Donal recalls that when his father, Dan William O'Driscoll, was not busy on the land he turned his hand to fishing. An early recollection is that of mackerel seine netting at small inlets on the west side of the island. He remembers the net

Donal O'Driscoll at his Castletownbere home, 2010.

as being extremely heavy. It was shot from a boat in semicircular fashion at the mouth of the inlet, thereby sealing it off as far as possible. The theory was that mackerel on the inside were then, for the most part, trapped. Ropes attached to the ends of the net were taken ashore to opposite sides of the inlet. What Donal remembers as an 'army of men' began to pull on the ropes in order to move the net towards the strand at the head of the inlet. All the while, another gang threw stones into the water in front of the net as it was being pulled inward. The purpose of the stone throwing was to divert fish into the net. As result of much pulling and hauling, the net was more or less brought ashore in the shallower water. Any spare men at hand began removing the trapped fish from the net. That was done by use of a large and more robust version of a kiddie's fishing net. It seems that this method of fishing was reasonably effective but extremely labour intensive. It did, however, have its limitations and could not be used at inlets with rocky seabeds. The net was prone to damage and frequently required repairing. That involved spreading it out in a field where the menders got to work with needles and twine. Donal recalls that the most proficient and fastest knitter by far in the O'Driscoll family was his sister Betty.

One of a family of fourteen children, six boys and eight girls, Donal was born in 1933. The boys eventually all followed the call of the sea and in time became high-profile fishermen. Donal remembers that he 'graduated' from lobster fishing in a punt to what he describes as his 'first real job; mackerel drift netting in Willie McCarthy's *Mystical Rose*, a boat of around 36 feet in length'. That, he says, 'was my first effort at going to sea'. His lasting memory of that particular venture is that the boat had a Bolinder engine fitted. It was a temperamental piece of machinery which he described in terms I can't really repeat here. Worst of all, from his viewpoint, he ended up the on-board engineer! That, he believes, was because no other crew member wanted the job. With the spring mackerel season lasting no more than four months, June 1950 marked the end of his tenure on the *Mystical Rose*.

During the summer of that year, Donal, aged seventeen, began to 'sub' or cover for absentee crew members on what he describes as 'Paddy O'Keeffe's boats'. Those boats were also variously referred to as 'Bigg's boats' (Bigg's being a company of which Paddy O'Keeffe was I believe chairman), 'Bantry boats', and 'Fastnet Fisheries boats' (Fastnet Fisheries being a subsidiary of Bigg's). The boats in question were named *Star of Meevagh, Deirdre, Joanna Mary* and *Marguerite*; four large trawlers by the standards of the time. Billy, Donal's brother was skipper of the *Star of Meevagh*, and another brother, Denis, was skipper of the *Marguerite*. Donal's 'subbing' lasted only a short time as he soon joined Billy on the *Star of Meevagh* as a permanent crew member. That he was a fast learner soon became obvious. Mind you, he did enjoy the advantage of having an exceptional tutor in his brother Billy; nevertheless the pupil had to be a bit special.

Marguerite, Donal's first boat, at Castletownbere regatta, 1962.

A reshuffle of skippers in the boats took place in 1952. It resulted in a vacancy for the position on the *Star of Meevagh*. Donal, then a mere nineteen-year-old, was, in his own words, 'called up before the green table and asked if I would consider taking the post'. It certainly speaks volumes for the esteem in which the young man was held and his ability as a fisherman, that a mature and astute businessman of Paddy O'Keeffe's calibre deemed him suitable to undertake a position of such immense responsibility. Donal went for it! Now, in hindsight, he says:

> I took the job in my innocence. It was a bit too soon; very trying for a young fellow. At that time you went out fishing in the morning and returned each evening. You were on your feet all day. When you are young you might not feel it a lot but on looking back it was a bit much. Anyway, I enjoyed it ... Someone recently asked me how fishermen cope with the hardships

associated with going to sea in all kinds of weather in order to make a living. My reply was, quite simply, you need to love the job! Perhaps that goes for every job to some extent, but where fishing is concerned it is absolutely essential. I loved my job.

Donal skippered the *Star of Meevagh* until around September 1954. In those times the 'Bantry boats' had a well-established schedule of fishing destinations throughout any particular year. They were to be found fishing out of Howth from early September to mid-November, from whence they turned their sights towards Helvick. Following a very short Christmas break at home they returned to Helvick, where they remained for a further five or six weeks. Mid-February saw the boats heading westwards and for the most part they fished out of Schull, Castletownbere or Bantry until late August.

While landings had been very good at Howth during the 1954 season, financial returns for fish were apparently not good. Poor prices led to low wages, which in turn led to discontent among the crews and eventually to an all-out strike. The response from the owners was to order the return of all four 'Bantry boats', and a fifth boat, the *Raingoose*, back to Bantry. The *Raingoose* was owned by Hanlon's Fish Merchants, Dublin, but managed by the Bantry-based company. The four 'Bantry boats' were secured at Bantry pier and put up for sale. Donal, along with his brothers Denis and Billy, were then for all intents and purposes no longer in employment. As such they approached BIM with the intention of putting their names down for a 50-footer. In the meantime, however, Paddy O'Keffee agreed to sell the *Marguerite* to the brothers. Consequently the notion of getting a 50-footer was dropped. The *Marguerite*, a 56ft Scotch-built boat, became the property of the O'Driscoll brothers in December 1954. Donal took on the role of skipper. Billy did likewise on the *Raingoose* and Denis purchased the Scotch-built *Loch Loy*. Over time, the remaining 'Bantry boats' were sold off; Mickey O'Donoghue, Bantry, former skipper of the *Joanna Mary* became her new owner, Ernie Adams, Skibbereen, bought the *Star of Meevagh*, and the *Deirdre* went to a retired Milford Haven trawler man, Bertie Hurst, who then lived locally. Peter Downey, Bantry, who had previously skippered the *Raingoose*, purchased the newly built BIM 50-footer *Ros Droichead*.

Donal very successfully fished the *Marguerite* up to 1964. He was mostly engaged in the whitefish sector. While he also spent a number of winters at Dunmore East herring fishing, he deemed the boat to be unsuitable for the catching technique used. His next boat, bought in partnership with his brother Michael Joe, was the 70ft *Honeydew*. Purchased from Francie West, Fraserburgh, in 1964, she was Scotch built and had up to then been a gill-netter. Donal fitted her out for trawling. He fished her up to the late 1960s, during which time, depending on location and time of year, she was to be found landing whitefish, prawns or herring. With the 1970s around the corner and the wonders of joining the EEC being widely publicised as our own specialist brand of utopianism, Donal joined the posse by deciding to replace the *Honeydew* with the *Marina,* a brand new 75ft Norwegian-built wooden vessel. Why not? When the brothers purchased the *Honeydew* in 1964, because she was Scotch built, the transaction did not qualify for government financial incentives granted towards the purchase of Irish-built boats. However, when the same partnership signed the dotted line for the *Marina*, in addition to a loan guaranteed by BIM, 25 per cent of the total cost was made available. Joe Joe O'Sullivan, another Castletownbere man, acquired the *Cisemair*, a virtual sister ship of the *Marina*, under the same terms. Both vessels were built at a boatyard near the southern Norwegian town of Flekkefjord. Donal took delivery of the 75ft *Marina* in August 1971. He describes her as, 'A lovely boat, a very handy little boat. The workmanship carried out on her was second to none.' At a later date she was re-engined at O'Donovan's Yard, Oldcourt. At the same time the original part-shelter-deck (whaleback) was replaced by a full version. Equipped for trawling and seining, the *Marina* engaged in lucrative fishing in the late 1980s when large quantities of quality hake were landed.

Casting his mind back over the years, Donal recalled that in the late 1940s and early '50s there was not a lot of money to be made out of fishing. That was certainly the case where fishermen were concerned, when £10 a week for a deckhand was regarded as 'very big money'. It was a time when fish were extremely plentiful. Very large catches were being landed at Howth. Presumably in an attempt to improve returns, fish was shipped across the Irish Sea via the *Raingoose* to Whitehaven. Yet, for

Marina (D532), *Honeydew II* (SO749) and Union Hall boat *Francis Maria* (D441), pictured in 2000, with Glandore, Co Cork in the background.

whatever reason, money filtering down to the crews was minuscule by any standards. It spawned a situation that led directly to the 'strike' already referred to.

So when and why did the lot of fishermen begin to improve? Well evidently it was something that evolved during the late 1950s and '60s. It was something that happened naturally, rather than the advent of any great masterplan. That particular period was one in which horizons in general began to expand. Mostly the incremental changes where fishing was concerned were quite small but each addition led to a forward step. Donal points out that in the days of the 'Bantry boats' marketing outlets were focused almost entirely on Cork and Dublin. As examples of how improvements began to come about he recalls that Hogg's, fish merchants from the west coast of Scotland, came to Castletownbere to buy fish which they exported to Spain. A few years later the co-ops began to form. While the co-ops were not initially involved in exporting, they were engaged in auctioning fish from the boats to buyers. That was an important development in the sense that previously buyers largely dealt directly with individual boats, the owners of which had to settle for whatever price was offered. The idea of open auctions carried out by co-op personnel introduced an element of competition among buyers that had previously not been there. There was, Donal says, 'good demand at that time, prices paid for herring were very good when compared to what you get now, especially when one considers the value of money'.

Donal's sons, Liam and Brendan, followed closely in their father's footsteps. Their livelihoods have been wholly linked with fishing. Not surprisingly, they both served their apprenticeships under the watchful eye of their parent maestro. They soon graduated to the rank of skippers, with Liam first taking charge of Joe Joe O'Sullivan's *Cisemair* (D533). Brendan's first boat was the 65ft Killybegs-built *Gerlisa* (SO446). Some years later he replaced her with the 1983 Baltimore-built 72ft *Honeydew II* (ex *Shay Og*) (SO749). Liam took over the *Marina* (D532) in 1991 when his father retired from fishing.

In the late 1990s, a family decision was taken to go for a half-and-half polyvalent pelagic vessel. That decision came to fruition in the form of the Swedish-built, steel-hulled, 90ft *Carmona* (S383). Both the *Marina* and *Honeydew II* were put up for sale and their tonnage went on to the *Carmona*. The vessel is currently fished by Liam and Brendan.

Donal's commitment to furthering the cause of Irish fishermen, particularly of those in the south-west, becomes evident when one considers the time and effort he has dedicated to various associated organisations. From the outset he was hugely instrumental in the formation of the Castletownbere Fishermen's Co-op in the 1960s. It's an organisation he was to chair for many years. Down through the decades he has been no

The *Carmona*. (Courtesy of David Linkie)

less involved in other prestigious organisations such as Irish Fish Producers' Organisation (IFPO), the Irish South & West Fishermen's Organisation (IS&WFO), and the Irish South & West Fish Producers Organisation (IS&WFPO). Indeed, he has held high office in each of those organisations and at all times has vigorously represented Irish fishermen.

It would be difficult to have a conversation with Donal without what must be the most dreaded topic in any Irish fisherman's psyche raising its head. It is, of course, that of the Common Fisheries Policy (CFP). His comment on it was, 'The dogs in the street know the CFP has been a despised strategy for many years and that it has come to be more so as time has gone on.' That view set the tone for the remainder of our chat on that topic.

It has to be borne in mind that it was in early June 2009 that I visited Donal. It was shortly after the Total Review of the CFP was announced. He was extremely sceptical that the slate will be wiped clean and that a completely fresh start will be made to sort out the mess that currently exists. He believes such an approach is vital. There is no point, he says, in any form of patchwork approach. He was deeply concerned that the open mindedness, the will, or indeed the real commitment required might not be there. Will the strong, opinionated individuals who at the end of the day make the important decisions listen to the stakeholders? Will *our* negotiators this time stand up for the rights of Irish fishermen as never before? Will all the stakeholders sing from the same hymn sheet? Will they make their voices heard in a way that will resound in corridors and boardrooms all the way to Brussels? Will those in authority whose brief it is to bring about what, in some quarters, will be unpopular decisions, have the courage and will to do so? Will it be recognised that mistakes were made over the past twenty-six years, and that while more stringent quotas were periodically introduced, fish stocks continued to diminish? Will lessons be learned from that scenario? There are so many questions that could be posed. Positive responses to the few highlighted here should go some way towards putting in place the changes so desperately needed.

Donal is strongly of the opinion that all twenty-seven EU countries should not be involved in decision-making where allocation of fish quotas for this country are concerned. He says:

> As the EU has expanded the situation has become so complicated that nobody knows where they are. For example, some Baltic countries have fishing fleets but they wouldn't be involved with this part of the world. They wouldn't have boats fishing here, we haven't boats fishing in their waters, so why should they have a say in what happens off the south-west coast of Ireland. In any case, as far as I'm aware, the Baltic fleets kept the entitlement they had previous to joining the EU. But crazy things happen – when Poland joined the EU its fleets were given a quota of 10,000 tonnes of mackerel; we couldn't get a mackerel for our small fleet here. Then Poland traded the allocation to Germany, who in turn seems to have made further arrangements with another country. It doesn't make sense.

So what is his proposal? It may well seem radical to many, but Donal's suggestion is that Ireland, the UK, France, Spain and Portugal – 'The Atlantic Arc' – should, through a combination of national control and bilateral agreements, be given ownership of the fishing rights adjacent to the Arc. In other words, those countries would have the opportunity of deciding what they want to do within their own area. He believes that the 200-mile limit should be reclaimed, with the first 50 miles adjacent to a particular state exclusive to it. The allocation of the remaining 150 miles would be a matter for agreement by the Arc countries. A smaller club with fewer people involved in decision-making should simplify matters. He believes, 'There is no other way stocks of fish are going to be saved and if it is not done now it will never happen.'

Another topic touched on was that of the Federation of Irish Fishermen (FIF). I asked Donal for his thoughts on the organisation. Did he believe that the umbrella organisation, formed in 2007, would be more effective than the separate entities in bringing the real needs of Irish fishermen to the table? Will FIF speak with a unified voice for the Irish fishing industry and offer an active input into policy-making decisions both nationally and internationally? His first reaction was to say, 'You would think it should be.' However, he felt that there was potential for a few problems, not least that it will be very hard to please everyone; within the federation the demands and requirements of each faction could differ considerably. He recalled, too, that in the not-too-distant past one of the main reasons the IS&WFPO came into being was because there was a perception that the Dublin-based IFPO was not serving the local fishermen as well as it might. Is there again a danger of overstretching in the sense of trying to do the impossible – being all things to all men? Donal believes so! Perhaps the idea of a rotating federation chairman between the CEOs of the four FPOs will, through time, lead to destabilisation. So is there still a strong case for each of the FPOs to go their own way? Yes, Donal believes there is!

Donal spent over forty years at sea. During those years he went from strength to strength by virtue of dedication, astuteness, attention to detail, keeping up with developments, and, above all, his outstanding ability to catch fish. When I asked if he recalled any specific incidents that had taken place over the years, he began by saying, 'Thank God, where we were concerned in the boats all went well. A crew member once injured his thumb; it was the worst that happened in any of my boats.' He did, however, recall one experience that took place when he was a very young man. The story went as follows:

A boat called the *Hidden Treasure*, property of O'Keeffe's, Bantry, was in Arklow being re-engined. My late brothers Billy and Denis, Fergus Williams, an engineer from Bantry, and myself set out from Bantry to bring the boat home. We travelled by lorry. Billy and Fergus were in the cab with the driver, while Denis, the engineer and I kept a punt company in the back. Strong east or south-east wind prevented us leaving Arklow for over a week. Even though there was still a strong breeze blowing, on a particular Sunday evening, we did eventually manage to get out over the bar. No sooner were we out than thick fog came down. Lo and behold the compass in the boat, which must have been in her since the year of dot, became unreadable. It was when the boat began to roll that the face of the compass became obscured by sediment. We didn't know whether we were going east or west! Billy was in charge in the wheelhouse and somehow found his way back into Arklow. We were there for another week!

At last decent weather came. We set out and everything seemed to be going grand. I wasn't used to being at sea much at that time and was feeling a bit sick so I went to lie down in a bunk. Next thing I knew there was commotion going on deep in the bowels of the boat. Soon it became apparent that the boat was making a considerable amount of water through the stern tube! Closer inspection by the men revealed that two bolts holding the stuffing box had sheared off. The water was in fact flooding in. We had just passed the Tuskar Rock Lighthouse and decided to head for Dunmore East. Even with the bilge pump constantly manned the water level continued to rise. We were the luckiest people in the world to make it ashore. That was my worst experience of a near miss.

Even though not directly involved, Donal also has vivid memories of one morning in the late 1950s, when the 62ft *Loch Loy* owned by his brother Denis hit a rock near Dursey Island. The boat quickly disintegrated. At the time of the accident only the *St Bernadette*, skippered by Gerry O'Shea, was in the vicinity. Before the remains of the boat sank, the crew managed to raise a flag of sorts. Fortunately, Gerry spotted it and reacted instantly. Thanks to his alertness the crew were taken off the wreck just before it disappeared beneath the waves. It is interesting to note how limited life-saving equipment on boats was at that time; a single rectangular tank stowed on top of the wheelhouse!

Hungry Hill, a Beara peninsula landmark and the highest peak in the Caha mountain range.

Denis had further bad luck with boats when on a winter's night in the 1970s, while herring fishing south of Toe Head, County Cork, his 75ft *Crystal River* went ashore on the Stags Rocks and became a total loss. Fortunately there was no loss of life.

Donal has reason to remember one particular morning when fishing out of Howth in the 1950s. He was skipper of the *Star of Meevagh* at the time. The morning was foggy and the *Raingoose*, skippered by Peter Downey, came up fairly close to Donal's boat. It was a kind of courtesy call to have a little chat without announcing to all and sundry over the radio how the fishing was going in the area. As the *Raingoose* began to move away, her shoulder (for want of a better term) tipped the stem post of the *Star of Meevagh* and knocked the post out sideways. She immediately began to make a lot of water. What was to be done? She was unlikely to make shore! Donal's brother, Billy, was also nearby in the *Deirdre*. Between them, the three skippers hatched up a plan to use the *Raingoose* and the *Deirdre* as a sort of raft by tying up at each side of the *Star of Meevagh*. Supported like so, the bold *Star* was floated into Howth.

The afternoon spent with Donal had flown. The time had come to take my leave from what had been a most enjoyable, interesting and informative session. As I drove homewards in the direction of Glengarriff, I felt obliged to get the camera out in an attempt to capture scraps of the idyllic surroundings. What a beautiful part of the world the Beara peninsula is on a sunny late afternoon!

BOAT LOADS OF FISH, DAY AFTER DAY

PEADAR O'NEILL OF ENNISCRONE, COUNTY SLIGO

The popular seaside village of Enniscrone, with its four miles of sandy beaches, is located on the shores of Killala Bay in west County Sligo. It is home to Peadar O'Neill. He first contacted me in 2008 to point out that I had omitted his ownership of the BIM 50-footer *Sancta Maria* from my writings on the histories of those particular boats. Well, as I explained to Peadar, it was one of those pieces of information that had not turned up during the research. It quickly transpired during the course of our conversation that Peadar was an amiable gentleman with a lifetime of fishing experiences behind him. As always, when a possible opportunity presents itself to chat with such a person, I asked if we could meet up sometime. 'No problem,' came the reply, 'anytime you're down this way just call in.' I took him at his word and was warmly welcomed by Peadar and his wife Celia at the O'Neill family home at Enniscrone in March 2009.

With the small talk over, Peadar began to recall information passed down by his predecessors, and to evoke occupational happenings during of his own lifetime. Fishing had been his main livelihood for the best part of fifty years or so.

Peadar O'Neill relaxing at his home in Enniscrone.

He began talking about what tough a business fishing on Killala Bay was, not only in his grandfather's time, but down to the early years of his own involvement. His grandfather fished a 28ft double-ended 'Greencastle boat' in an era before engines of any sort were available. He carried out the very skilled operation of trawling by sail power as far away as Lackan Bay, on the outer reaches of Killala Bay. Peadar's father also sail-trawled for a number of years before old lorry engines began to be fitted in boats. By all accounts there were times when those troublesome old pieces of machinery almost led to people lamenting the demise of the sail.

It is almost inconceivable nowadays, but Peadar remembers a time when the pier at Enniscrone was in such a poor state of repair that for safety reasons, fishing boats had to be taken ashore and launched on a daily basis. Those operations, which took place during the fishing season, entailed the removal of all gear and ballast each evening before the boats were hand winched ashore, and replacement of the same when boats were refloated the following morning. Having gone through that procedure there was every possibility that the engine wouldn't start without a great deal of coaxing, and when it did, the Worton Blake water-cooling pump could well refuse to function. But deliverance from the misery was at hand in the form of Lister diesel engines. As Peadar put it, 'The Lister diesel engine was a gift, it gave no problem at all.'

The main kind of fishing carried out around Killala Bay in the 1950s was trawling. Peadar recalls:

We were getting loads of turbot, brill, sole and skate. Turbot weighing up to 20lbs and sole the length of your arm was not unusual. There was fish for the world and little or no price being paid for it. We used to land five or six boxes per day. Now you could spend a whole day out there and you wouldn't get enough for your dinner. It was the same with lobsters but we were too busy trawling to fish them. As result of being pestered by a man from Ballina who was always looking for lobsters, we did shoot a dozen pots at the back of the pier on our way out one morning. We hauled them on our return that evening; there were eighteen lobsters in the twelve pots. Marketing fish was cumbersome, we used to sell some on the pier but most of it went to M. & P. Hanlon's, Fish Merchants, Dublin. My late uncle used to take it to the railway station in Ballina by means of an ass and cart.

When his father retired, Peadar took over the boat and continued the practices learned from 'the boss' over the years. He had been a good student, one who had taken a keen interest not only in the various facets of actual fishing but also in the preparation of first-class fishing gear. Indeed, the young pretender, who was adept at making trawls, claims that with the help of a BIM course and ideas of his own, he actually improved on the fishing potential of gear used.

As has been the case in so many west-coast ports, salmon fishing has long been at the heart of the culture and livelihood of Enniscrone dwellers. Anchored nets were used in the early days. Peadar was part of a four-man crew in a 24ft boat. It was, he said:

> ...a tough job rowing, one that has left me, as it did my father, with a lump on my hand. Thankfully the Seagull outboard engine came on the market before too long. It was not, however, the complete answer. Indeed, it was a very temperamental piece of machinery; it would break your heart at times.

As the post-war years wore on, there was a general tendency to move away from the more laborious and troublesome aspects of work. Fishing was no exception; modern boats with inboard engines soon came on the scene.

Topical at the time in the Enniscrone area was a legal case to establish whether anchored nets in Killala Bay were fixed or stationary. Not surprisingly, it was the landlords who simply didn't want fishermen using nets of any kind that took the fixed-net stance. Fishermen who argued that nets free to move through 360 degrees could not be regarded as fixed won the case. As time moved on, the era of the fixed net largely faded out and it was replaced by the cotton drift net. Until the arrival of the even more effective nylon nets they fished mostly at night. The drift nets, Peadar says, 'were far more effective than the fixed version that swung around through 360 degrees allowing all sorts of debris to become tangled in them'.

Around the mid-1960s, at a time when salmon and herring fishing was a lucrative business on the Donegal, Sligo and Mayo coasts, Peadar decided to get a bigger boat. With that aspiration in mind, he attended a course in Dún Laoghaire which led to the awarding of a skipper's ticket. He then decided to purchase a BIM 50-footer, the procuring of which led him to Howth, where the excellently maintained *Sancta Maria* was up for sale. He brought the trawler home and began fishing her out of Sligo. That was, of course, a change of base, since Peadar had previously worked out of Enniscrone. But it had to be done as the facilities at Enniscrone were inadequate for the larger boat, and also Sligo was more central both for access to the fishing grounds and for transportation of fish to markets.

A watercolour painting of the *Sancta Maria*.

At that time Peadar held a license to legally fish salmon anywhere within the area south of a line from St John's Point on the Donegal coast right across to Erris Head on the north-west extremity of County Mayo. During the summer months he concentrated largely on drift netting off Mullaghmore.

His memories of herring fishing in the winters of 1967, '68, '69 and '70 are, 'of boat loads of fish day after day. The channel up to Sligo was full of herring.' Peadar's routine was to go down to the last buoy out off Rosses Point around 10 a.m. and shoot the trawl. The trick, he says, was:

…to shoot it when heading for Rosses Point. As you came in towards the shore there was a deep hole in the seabed. You carried on in until you were so close in that the trawl door could be seen rising as the net came up out of the hole. The next thing you saw was this enormous white mound behind you; the net would be full to the lip with herring. Two such tows filled the boat and we were back up in Sligo by 4 p.m.

I couldn't help thinking that the often maligned lack of draught associated with the BIM 50-footers had to be the key to working so close to the shore. When I mentioned as much to Peadar he completely agreed, and added that it was great because it kept the bigger Killybegs boats with greater draught away from that particular patch. The water was too shallow for them to operate in.

When I enquired about markets for what must have been considerable quantities of herring, Peadar recalled that he sent a lorry load to Molloy's, Fish Merchants, Dublin, four times per week. Most of the fish were sold for around £3 per cran. Whenever there was a glut the only outlet was the fish meal factory at Killybegs. Herring were so plentiful that some people were not as careful as they might have been when dealing with the fish. It could be said that an overabundance led to carelessness and consequently abuse of a natural resource. Peadar says, 'The herring used to disappear over night, there was loads of them one day, the next day they were gone. From 1971 onwards herring became very scarce around here. Trawling for whitefish then became our main thing.'

In the early 1970s, when boat owners were being encouraged to purchase larger boats, Peadar gave the idea some considerable thought. Along with the likes of Killybegs men Albert Swan, Tommy Watson and the McCalligs, he listened as BIM personnel explained the advantages. Indeed, he agrees that the packages and terms on offer were very good, and that financially it probably would have been a good move. His main problem was that if he was to step up from the 50-footer to a larger vessel, it would mean a move of base from Sligo to Killybegs. That in turn meant uprooting his wife and then family of three from Enniscrone. That, he said, 'would be a very big upheaval; you don't like going away from the place you were brought up in and leaving behind the people you knew all your life'. In the end Peadar decided to stay put and he fished the 50-footer for a few more years. As time went on it became an extremely onerous job, 'I became a sort of itinerant; constantly on the go.' The routine was to leave home on Sunday night, drive to Ballina, load the trailer with boxes of ice, travel on to Sligo, put the ice and water on board, leave for the fishing grounds around 4 a.m., fish all day, go into Killybegs on Monday night, get more ice and a bit of food, spend a few hours in the bunk, head out again, and fish right through until around 1 p.m. on Wednesday. Then it was back to Sligo, pack the fish, arrange for a CIE lorry to take the fish to the station, load the fish onto the lorry and then return home by road to Enniscrone. There were times, he says:

> …when I was so tired that I didn't remember driving home. After a while it became clear that my health wouldn't stand up to that lifestyle and it was then I decided to sell the *Sancta Maria*. She was well equipped when I sold her and her engine had recently undergone a major overhaul at the hands of that genius of an engineer, Jack McGee. When he had finished I asked if I should drive her easy for a while. Jack's reply was, 'Jesus Christ man, what do you think, after all my trouble doing a first-class job? Take her easy indeed; drive her flat out, as hard as she can go.'

Peadar's lifelong association with fishing continued, but in a less stressful mode. He replaced the *Sancta Maria* with a 26ft fibreglass vessel and worked out of Enniscrone. He still has the boat and even though there is virtually no fish to be caught in Killala Bay now, he occasionally goes out during the summer in the hope of getting a few mackerel. Sadly, he believes that as far as one can tell at this point in time, 'Fishing in Killala Bay, at one time one of the best bays in Ireland for flat fish, is finished.' So where did it all go wrong? According to Peadar:

> The reasons are multiple: fishing gear became too sophisticated, fish-finding technology and associated aids reached unbelievable levels, and fishermen became ultra clever at maximising the advantages at their disposal. Additionally, let's not forget the damage done by tangle nets and by immature fish not being returned to the sea. Whatever genius came up the tangle net idea is responsible for killing millions of fish on their very own breeding grounds. Boats were landing up to 150 boxes of turbot per shot. It couldn't last.

When I asked Peadar if he remembered any unusual happenings during his long fishing career, he thought a little before admitting that there was one occasion when he was really frightened. He related the following account:

One day we were out salmon fishing. Without warning a mighty swell came out of nowhere. In a short time the seas became mountainous. We were heading up Killala Bay towards Enniscrone in the fibreglass boat I have now. I made contact on the radio with a boat that had gone in ahead of us to be told that conditions were very bad at the pier; a boat had already broken away. In the meantime there were three or four ferocious waves towering in astern of us, I had never seen the likes of it and I had been fishing a long time! It was the first and only time I was ever frightened in a boat. We had no hope of going into Enniscrone and were advised if possible to head for Killala. The problem was that if I had attempted to turn the boat she would certainly have capsized or have been swamped. I had an experienced man with me whom I asked to keep an eye out for a lull of any sort in the waves coming behind us. A chance came and eventually with plenty to do I managed to turn the boat towards Killala. Getting in there wasn't easy but we made it eventually. There had to be some kind of under sea eruption to cause such mountainous waves.

The golden beaches of Enniscrone. (Courtesy of Eugene Dolan, Dublin)

It had been great talking with Peadar. Time was getting on and anyway, the man had other matters to attend to. Yes indeed, he is a keen and reportedly accomplished set dancer. Later that evening the tall, slim, fit, seventy-year-old had an important engagement to fulfil. A final and significant remark made by Peadar was, 'Fishing was very good to me. Maybe I didn't exactly make a fortune, but my family have all done very well for themselves.'

While I had been chatting to Peadar, Una took the opportunity of doing some local sightseeing. She was highly impressed by the golden, sandy beaches and sussed out the very impressive Diamond Coast Hotel, where we had an evening meal before heading off to Galway.

Sadly I have to report that since my visit to Peadar at Enniscrone, his wife, Celia, the lovely lady I met on that occasion, passed away following a short illness. My deepest sympathy goes out to the O'Neill family.

I WAS AMBITIOUS AND BECAME IMPATIENT

GERRY O'SHEA OF HOWTH, COUNTY DUBLIN

With memories of Christmas and New Year festivities fading fast, Una and I decided to alleviate the winter blues by taking a February trip to Dublin. Whilst there I took the opportunity of travelling out to Howth in order to meet up with Gerard (Gerry) O'Shea, a gentleman I had been trying to track down for a long time. His wife, Mary, kindly offered to collect me at the Dart Station. I was to give her a ring when I arrived there. Alas, for whatever reason, maybe I wrote the phone number down incorrectly or used the wrong code, I don't really know, but I failed to make the prearranged contact. I tend to have problems with telephones!

However, Howth is not that big; a few enquires soon had me on the way to Coolcour, Kilrock Road. While still some distance from the house, I spotted Gerry inspecting garden shrubbery. The chances are that he was wondering, 'Where's that fellow who was to phone half an hour ago?' Nevertheless, he greeted me warmly, invited me in, and introduced me to Mary. With the pleasantries over it was the lifetime experiences of the now retired but eminent fisherman that we began to talk about. Currently an octogenarian, Gerry grew up as part of a large family on the outskirts of Castletownbere, County Cork. It was during the harsh times of the 1930s that he first came face-to-face with the realities of life. Yet the O'Shea home was a happy one. There were no frills, but there was a caring family and always plenty of food on the table.

Gerry believes that the current economic downturn and perceived related hardships are minuscule when compared with those of the 1930s. What happened then, he says, was twofold:

> Firstly, social security fell down because the government didn't have the money to pay out dole, and secondly, the fallout arising from disagreements between the government of our country and that of the UK led to a situation whereby farm produce markets, including cattle, completely disappeared.

Gerry O'Shea, 2009.

Gerry O'Shea in his younger days.

He went on to say, 'The mountains and fields were chock full of what had become worthless animals.' With the consequences of such catastrophic happenings taking their toll on everyday life, and the Second World War rampant, Gerry left school and began fishing with his uncles. That was in 1942. He didn't know it then, but from such humble beginnings he was to go on to become a first-rate fisherman. His life story is indeed a story of success!

His uncles' half-decker, the *Grove*, was fitted with a 13/15hp engine. The power generated was probably no less than could be expected, nevertheless, when towing a trawl, Gerry recalls putting his hand over the side of the boat and touching the water to check that there was forward motion. Lack of power meant that fishing had to be done at night because in daylight the fish would swim away from the trawl. Gerry says:

> Fish were solid – loads of plaice and other flat fish everywhere. We used to get a box or so per hour. Selling it was a problem, but my grandmother, who lost her husband in a drowning accident, and yet became a great business-woman in later life, used to take the fish to the market in Kenmare. She would take about eight boxes on a Thursday. That was a lot of fish then. We fished for herring from October to February, catching thirty to forty boxes a week. That was a good living.

As result of the years spent with his uncles, the fact that commercial fishing had considerable potential dawned on Gerry. However, that potential was not going to be realised fishing out of Castletownbere in a half-decker. He would have to move on if he was to better himself. In 1947, aged nineteen, he took the plunge and headed off for Milford Haven, Wales. He went on a deep-sea trawler as a crew member. It was a job that would see him fish not only around home shores but also to experience the unsympathetic conditions of Icelandic and Bear Island waters.

Having spent three years based at Milford Haven, during which time he was joined by his brother Sean, Gerry's next move was to the Lancashire seaport of Fleetwood on the west coast of England. The steep learning curve he experienced at those vibrant fishing ports was to influence the remainder of his fishing career. As he put it:

The *Ros Beara*. (Courtesy of Stuart Emery, Leigh-on-Sea)

> I knew that fishing could be a very big thing but at the time I couldn't get anyone in Castletownbere interested in backing me to buy a big boat. People didn't want to know anything about it. Fishing was regarded as a subsistence business as far as they were concerned.

However, he was determined to go it alone and with Sean's help he gathered up the £700 deposit required to procure the 50ft *Ros Beara*. The boat was delivered in the summer of 1955. She was, he says, 'A grand little boat.'

Gerry returned to fish off Castletownbere and in Kenmare Bay but never really settled on the south coast. From a booming Fleetwood he had returned to a situation where markets were extremely poor and incentives to remain fishing out of his home town were scant. He recalls that period as follows:

We started seine netting. Haddock were the main catch. There were times when we didn't get a shilling a box clear. I gave up the seine netting and went trawling in Kenmare Bay. It was more lucrative – ten or so boxes of flatfish were landed per twenty-four hours. However, I quickly saw that I wasn't going to make much money fishing out of Castletownbere. I was ambitious and became impatient, feeling that things were not moving fast enough. I moved to Howth, where we were getting eight shilling a box for whiting; we were making money at that. Ten shillings a box was big money in Howth because of its proximity to the Dublin market. In Castletownbere it was nothing when transport and other expenses were paid.

He lamented the drawbacks of that distance factor, because, as he said, 'I used to tell people that the turbot were dying of old age in Kenmare Bay; they weren't getting caught. The young fellows used to laugh when I told them.'

Gerry acquired a second boat in the late 1950s. It partly came about because the *Ros Beara* was damaged in a collision while fishing in Dunmore East. While waiting for the damage to be sorted out Gerry was without a boat. Knowing that there was an unallocated BIM 56-footer going spare, he approached the Board and suggested that he would take her. That's how he became owner of the second boat, *St Bernadette*. He retained ownership of the *Ros Beara* and in fact became owner of two further boats, the *San Patricio* (*Ploughboy*) and the *Primula*, in a three-year spell around that time.

By the early 1960s, the Irish fishing fleet had grown enormously and as the decade progressed, it continued to grow. 'Too big for its boots,' Gerry says. He recalls that when he first started landing at Howth around 1956/57 there was a good living to be made. It was helped by the fact that at times during the winter, south-west gales kept the boats of the south and west coast tied up, while on the sheltered east coast fishing continued. But that didn't last. As the boat numbers grew the Dublin Fish Market was permanently over supplied. There was virtually no fish exported at the time. As an example of the situation that existed Gerry quoted the following:

I once landed over one hundred boxes of fish that included eight boxes of plaice, three boxes of prawn tails and the remainder of good cod. The entire catch made just over £100. Next day the buyers rang me to say the boxes were slack because ice had been put on the fish. The market was just terrible.

He continued:

A strike which took place because of low prices made no difference. A point was reached during one winter (October to March) when I lost £2,500. That was the cue to start selling off the boats. It was a hard decision, as my brother Sean was skipper of one and another brother, Willie, fished in the *San Patricio*. Yet, the fact was, had the boats been tied up I'd have been £2,500 better off.

With the *Ros Beara*, *St Bernadette*, and *San Patricio* sold off, Gerry was then left with only the more recently acquired *Salto*.

Some time later, while on a visit to Holland, he noticed how well the 'beamers' were doing over there. It was then that it occurred to him that

The *Salto*.

that was the direction in which he should go. Without any more ado he bought a steel-built Dutch beamer, the *Marie Jacob*, and went sole fishing in Morecambe Bay on the north-west coast of England. He knew that particular kind of fishing would be good because of previous experiences when working with ordinary trawls. It was an instant success! Alas, in a short time his arrangement with a fish company at the Dublin market to buy his fish collapsed. This time it was 270 boxes of prime fish at stake. Outlets simply didn't exist for quantities of that magnitude. It was then that he turned his attention towards landing and marketing his fish at Fleetwood. From then on, I believe it could be said that he never looked back. His last landing of fish in an Irish port took place in 1971.

At Fleetwood he linked up with the Boston Deep Sea Fishing Company, an agency that looked after not only the marketing of fish but also the facilities required in order to maximise fishing efficiency. As Gerry puts it:

> The Boston Deep Sea Fishing Company was a big trawling company. They had arrangements with buyers that were better than the open market. Expenditure incurred in the way of food, fuel or gear, for example, at any port on the Irish Sea or west coast of Scotland was simply charged to Boston. Of course, there was a fee to pay for the service but if you paid the bill within thirty days you got 2½ per cent off. It was great for me. Landing and marketing large quantities of fish, at times maybe 200 boxes of sole, was no longer a problem. They were great times; we lived like lords on the boats.

Gerry's fishing activities continued to go from strength to strength, so much so, that in over a thirty-year period, the *Marie Jacob* was replaced by a second and a third *Marie Jacob*. All three were Dutch-built beamers. The boats were getting bigger and better all the time. A measure of just what a great fisherman Gerry was can be gleaned from past copies of the *Fleetwood Chronicle*. It ran a column that listed boats' earnings. The *Marie Jacob* headed those lists over a three to four year period with such frequency that envious local fishermen claimed she should not be included because the skipper was not a Fleetwood man. They eventually got their way! As an afterthought Gerry recalled that, 'Our best week's wages on the last *Marie Jacob* was £4,000.'

Marie Jacob II.

Gerry openly admits that he was not an easy skipper to sail with. His expectations of crew performance and dedication were very high. He obviously didn't suffer fools lightly. Nevertheless he believes that he treated the men well and is proud of the fact that a number of them fished with him for over thirty-five years. He recalls how fortunate he was to have, over the years, men of the calibre of Gregory Conneely, the late Kevin McHugh, Willie Devanney, Mick Doyle and Teddy, his own brother. Gerry fished until around 1999, and on his retirement, Willie Devanney, one of the thirty-five-year crew men, took over as skipper of the *Marie Jacob*.

Before I parted company with Gerry he related memories from his early life on the Beara peninsula. He remembered that when fishing with his uncles in the *Grove*, as well as trawling and herring fishing, they also dredged for scallops. They worked grounds around Valencia Island and south of Scull, as well as off Castletownbere. The dredges were made by a local blacksmith. He reckoned that the non-rigid ones, without rivets,

Marie Jacob III.

were the best. That type was more pliable and fished better as a result. Dredging, he says, 'was hard work; we had no winch which meant the gear had to be hand hauled'.

As the eldest boy in a family of eight children, four boys and four girls, life in those frugal days has obviously stayed with him. He remembers that his father, a shoemaker, actually brought home less than £2 per week:

> We lived in a newly built corporation house. There was an acre of land going with it. That was the best acre of land ever known. With an acre of land you could grow all you needed. Then you had a bog, everyone had a bog in the mountain. You didn't actually own the bog but you paid the man that owned it so much a load for the turf. We had lots of fish, and three or four families could buy a skinned calf between them for ten shillings. A butcher from Bantry came along and cut it up. There was no point in rearing cattle because there was no market, so they killed the animals off at calf stage. Yes, we lived well but we had no money.

He laughed as he recalled one incident from his childhood days, 'A French fishing boat was brought into Castletownbere where it had its gear confiscated for illegal fishing. The local people were so concerned for the poor French fishermen that a collection was taken up and given to them so that they could buy their gear back.' How times have changed! While on the subject of French fishermen, Gerry also recalled that they used buy some of those unwanted cattle that roamed the lands and cut them up for lobster-pot bait. That, of course, was before it was discovered that beef was deadly bait for lobsters.

Well, while Gerry didn't exactly start off at the rags stage he certainly made it all the way to the riches category through good business acumen, ambition, determination and above all an extraordinary talent for harvesting the seas. As he drove me back to the Dart Station on that February day, he mentioned that the *Marie Jacob* (Mark 1) was the first beamer on the Irish coast. Reading between the lines from other remarks he made on the way, I believe that he was highly regarded in Dutch fishing ports where he regularly landed. He mentioned too that while Howth is now home, along with Mary and members of a now extended family, he frequently returns to their spacious holiday home in Castletownbere. I'd spent about three hours listening to Gerry's interesting life story. Unfortunately it's difficult to retain all one is told, you feel like going back again to recap odds and ends. Maybe I will one day – that's if he'll have me!

IT'S ALL SO DISHEARTENING

MICK ORPEN OF CASTLETOWNBERE, COUNTY CORK

It was on a really fine Saturday morning in early July 2009 that I set out on the journey from Ballycastle to West Cork. On the way I stopped off briefly at Tullamore. There, at the revamped and highly impressive O'Connor Park, I watched the interesting McCarthy Cup hurling qualifier between Cork and Offaly. With the evening-start match over, I drove on to Innishannon and spent the night with my nephew Jim and his wife Colette. The fact that Jim was a Cork senior football team selector greatly heightened interest in the Munster final to be played at Pairc Ui Caoimh the following day. Colette, son Shane, and I for obvious reasons had the best seats in the house! With the match result going our way, a pleasant and most enjoyable evening/night was had by all. Monday saw me heading further south to Union Hall, where I visited my brothers and their families. The next day I had an important engagement to fulfil at Castletownbere. Yes, it was a previously arranged meeting with experienced and well-known fisherman Michael (Mick) Orpen.

Over the years, the wondrous westward drive from Bantry has lost none of its charm. The magnificence of the bay, the beauty of Glengarriff's stunning surroundings, and the widespread rugged splendour of the expansive Beara peninsula captivates in a special way. On the outskirts of the widely known

West Cork fishing port, a right turn off the main road took me in the direction of Derrymihan West. After a wee bit of searching, the Orpen family home materialised. Out to greet me came Mick, a man I first came to know almost sixty years ago when he came to Baltimore as a seventeen or eighteen-year-old crewman on the *Marguerite*, a boat then owned by Bigg's, Bantry. Indeed, I well remember that along with up to twenty teenagers, and others well past that age, we spent many a Sunday afternoon playing football at Baltimore pier on the concrete, one-time mackerel processing area adjacent to Skinner's Boatyard. I do believe that he donned the local club jersey on a few occasions. But was he a registered player? Of course not, but that was of little consequence in the depths of West Cork in the early 1950s. I do hope objections will not be forthcoming from Castlehaven, Skibbereen, Goleen, Newcestown or other local GAA clubs on the strength of my disclosure! Ah yes, those were the days; all so long ago. In the intervening years Mick has become a highly respected household name in commercial fishing circles nationwide. Through his various experiences while skippering the five or six boats he came to own, he has seen it all; the good, the bad and the ugly.

Mick was born into a large Bere Island family. As with all areas of rural Ireland in the 1930s and '40s, times were tough. He recalls that the army were then based on the island and that personnel were generous in helping out with items of clothing. That, he says, 'helped immensely'. After leaving school he went fishing, because as he says, 'There wasn't much else to do.' He added, 'Scallop fishing in the winter months was good and the only earner.'There used to be three of a crew in the boat which was either a punt or yawl. Interestingly, the method of quantifying scallops was the same as that used for mackerel, i.e. three to a cast, forty-two cast to a hundred, etc.When it came to marketing scallops, Mick explained that they were very perishable fish and had to be packed in small numbers in dampened coarse bags.They were then transported by road to Bantry, put on a train to Cork, where along with fish from Schull, Cahirciveen, Dingle, Baltimore, Union Hall and other ports they were loaded into a container. The container was then put on to the cross-channel ferry vessel *Innisfallen* for shipping to Fishguard. From there it was transferred to the Billingsgate Market, London. All this took place within a twenty-four-hour period!

Mick at his Castletownbere home, 2009.

Mick spent a couple of seasons scallop fishing before joining the crew of the aforementioned *Marguerite*. It seemed like the right thing to do at the time. There was a perception that fishing on what were regarded as big boats could be lucrative. Perhaps Mick made his move at the wrong time, because shortly afterwards, when fishing out of Howth, the crew of the *Marguerite,* along with their counterparts on three other boats belonging to the same owners, went on strike. Why? Because they felt they were not getting a fair share of returns for fish landed. As a result of the strike, on orders of the owners, the boats ceased to fish. Mick was out of a job.

Where to next? Well, he boarded the *Innisfallen* and tried his luck in England. Sadly that didn't work out because he was too young; employers wouldn't take him on. By the time he returned to Ireland six months later, the then Sherkin Island O'Driscoll brothers, Billy, Denis and Donal had purchased the *Marguerite*. Mick rejoined the crew. That was to be his source of employment for a number of years, during which he experienced trawling and seining out of Castletownbere and Dunmore East.

Eventually Mick decided to get his own boat. He went for one that was up for sale at Dunmore East. She was called the *Intrepid*. The name suggests that she was fearless, valiant, heroic and gallant, but she didn't really live up to any of those adjectives, at least not during Mick's stewardship. Reputedly, the Danish-built boat was very successful in her early days but the big-hearted Castletownbere man says, 'She was not successful for me, and the simple reason was you couldn't keep her afloat. She would be alright lying beside the pier but when out fishing she leaked like a basket. Her problems didn't end there. Mick described her 88hp Kelvin engine as 'a menace'. He went on to say:

> I cursed it every time we had to start it. If it didn't go first time you'd had it. Nearly everyone of those Kelvins blew up for one reason or another. Gardners were completely different. They were good industrial engines and easy to maintain. She also had a rather odd gearbox. You had to check before you came into port as to whether it was stuck in gear or not.

With a roguish smile Mick added, 'I must have been very innocent when I bought her; there was little or nothing in the way of navigational aids in her.' Yet, in spite of the various drawbacks experienced with the *Intrepid*, Mick fished her for a few years out of a number of ports, including Milford Haven. Eventually she was scrapped. Mind you, he found a market for that much maligned 88hp Kelvin!

Mick next considered the possibility of getting a BIM 50-footer. Disappointingly his application fell on deaf ears. In hindsight he believes that was a blessing in disguise. Fishing was what he knew and it continued to be his way of life. Following the scrapping of the *Intrepid* he fished on trawlers out of Grimsby and Hull. Then a temporary change in employment took him off to the USA, where he worked in construction for a few years. While at that stage he seemed to have travelled far and experienced much, he was still only in his mid-twenties. Fate was to determine a return to Bere Island. While still in the USA his father became ill and Mick was asked to return home. With a fishing career still foremost on his mind, in partnership with local men Gerald McCarthy and Donal Murphy, he got what he describes as his 'first real boat', the Scotch-built *Silver Dawn*.

Ever forward-looking, Mick got wind of a 70ft boat for sale in Scotland. Word came through James Moriarity, a BIM executive, who offered financial help with the purchase should Mick be interested. A visit to Scotland proved fruitful, as the *Ardent* (S23), a four-year-old seiner built by Jones, Buckie, was in excellent condition. She was just what Mick had in mind and proved to be a very good boat in every way. He fitted her out for trawling and fished her very successfully on the south and east coasts until 1974. She was then sold on to a Dunmore East man. Later, when Dingle based, she was lost off the Kerry coast.

Ardent II (S23), built at Baltimore in 1974.

The 86ft Dutch-built *Ardent Again* (S23).

By 1974, Ireland had joined the EEC and the scent of wine and roses brought to the Irish fishing industry by that union may have just begun to fade a little. However, with funding of at least 50 per cent of the total cost of boats still on offer to virtually all and sundry, it's no wonder that Mick joined the merry throng and went for the first brand new 80ft boat built at the Baltimore BIM yard. The name *Ardent* (S23) was retained. Initially engine teething problems laid her up for six months or so, but as he put it, 'She fished very well after'. Misadventure led to her loss off the Old Head of Kinsale while herring fishing in 1984.

In time, Mick got back in business with the bigger and better boat named *Ardent Again* (S23). The 1967 Dutch-built, steel-hulled, 86ft vessel proved a great success. However, *tempus fugit*, and the next generation of Orpens were arriving on the scene. With sons Johnny, Eamonn and Michael all showing a keen interest in fishing, it was inevitable the they would follow in their father's footsteps and carry on the lifestyle he had worked so diligently to establish. Today Johnny fishes yet another *Ardent*, an 80ft vessel that arrived at Castletownbere in the early 2000s. Along with her came several other vessels as part of the government's renewal programme. Castletownbere was by then firmly established as the largest whitefish port in the country, with landings being valued at £15 million. Eamonn and Michael junior currently fish the polyvalent vessel *Guiding Star II*.

The current *Ardent*, fished by Mick's son Johnny.

The *Ardent* and *Guiding Star II*.

Over the years Mick has been no shrinking violet where matters relating to the Irish fishing industry are concerned. Nothing has changed! He has always, without fear or favour, called a spade a spade and is severely critical of where the Common Fisheries Policy has led us. He is especially critical of negotiators from this country, who he believes have again and again failed miserably to further the cause of Irish fishermen. He goes on to comment on the failures, weaknesses and lost opportunities ever prevalent in the management of the industry as a whole, 'The fisheries that surround this island nation were amongst our greatest assets. Alas, they are largely no longer ours! Surely that's a serious indictment on those in whom we placed our trust in government and in those who went to fight our corner in Brussels and elsewhere.'

He laments the giveaways to the EU and the miserable scraps that have come our way in return. He is critical of the ways in which marketing abroad and processing in this country have been handled. He is bitterly disappointed by the manner in which men carrying out what he describes as the most unsociable job in the world, often in horrendous conditions, have been criminalised. He doubts that those in authority have any understanding of what being thrown about while standing at the wheel of a boat for up to ten hours in poor weather conditions does to a man; a man that has to remain vigilant throughout for the sake of his own boat, the boats of others, his gear and above all the safety of his crew. He wonders if the fisheries officer sent out by his/her boss to do a job appreciates that a tired man at midnight on the high seas may well make mistakes in entries to that log book on which so much emphasis is now placed. He feels strongly that as in other countries, breaches of laws relating to illegal fishing should be dealt with in a way that does not make criminals out of hard-working men; there are plenty of other ways those matters could be dealt with. Take Norway for instance, a country with a population similar to that of Ireland and one that has a thriving fishing industry. Surprise, surprise it is not a member of the EU. Why? Because not once but twice fishermen gave a firm 'no' when confronted with referenda on entry, i.e. no outside control. So what have they? A yearly set price for fish, fisheries and a fishing industry efficiently controlled and managed by authorities who are agreeably advised by their own fishermen and scientists. The results are fisheries littered with fish, happy fishermen and an industry that stands side by side with that of oil and gas. As for illegal fishing, fishermen are, of course, rightly penalised when offences occur, but they are not criminalised.

The intensity with which the following passage was spoken gave an immense insight into how unhappy Mick is with the way things have gone,

Fishermen are not treated fairly! I'm sorry to say I have three lads fishing at the moment. The regulations they have to comply with, the bookwork they have to contend with and the deterrents against them are inhuman. Fishermen are not happy! To cap it all markets prices are against them. Fish is being imported into this country without proper traceability or testing for human consumption. The minister says that nothing can be done about imports. What a sad state of affairs that is. It's all so disheartening. I don't know where fishermen get the heart to continue. I suppose they are caught in a trap, Johnny's boat cost £4 million. If I was a young man I wouldn't do it, I just *would not do it*.

Mick continued:

While the fishermen in this country are hounded and restricted in virtually every way possible, off the west coast of Ireland you have gigantic factory ships, out of Holland mostly, fishing as happily as you like. They are taking fish of all sizes and kinds aboard, putting them through a screener where only one size is retained. Those retained eventually go to market; the remainder are made into fish meal. The amount of fish one of those ships can freeze in comparison to our boats is enormous. Back at home those ships have back-up refrigerated factory facilities where fish is stored, possibly further processed, and generally made ready for marketing. It's another world. It baffles me. I can't understand how it's allowed to happen.

Those are the words of Mick Orpen!

Next on the agenda were Mick's thoughts on the ongoing/upcoming Common Fisheries Review. He wondered if those in authority in this country really cared about the industry, or indeed if they have given up the ghost on what some see as an irreversible situation. Should those observations be incorrect and if a serious effort is to be made to salvage something from the shambles, then he has suggestions to make. However difficult it may be, he says:

Every effort should be made to avoid a patchwork solution. In as far as possible clean the slate; start all over. We are talking about a total review, therefore our negotiators with the strength of our government behind them have to be seen to stand up against their counterparts from other member states; be strong. No matter how unpopular demands on limits, quotas, etc., may be, they have to stand firm and not allow others to brush them aside. Don't take no for an answer. Before sending negotiators out on their mission, our government should follow the example of other EU countries and along with regular advisors involve those who have worn their teeth at the sharp end of the fishing industry. Those without whom an industry such as it now is would not exist. Six fishermen, two from the deep water sector, two from the mid-water sector and two from the inshore sector should be conscripted so that the benefits of their enormous experiences and wisdom can be taken to the negotiating table … It's no good saying it's a dead duck; that all was sold out in 1972. Our negotiators will have to get in there and do their jobs, that is what they are there for and no other country is going to help our cause. We will have to step up to the plate and find our own solutions. If it is not done this time around the whole thing will be gone and there will be nothing left to negotiate. It is clear that we are not going to get everything back but we can't be seen to be giving, giving all the time. What we want for a start off is a fair share of our own waters, that may include a limits change, and unlikely as it may seem now, no stone should be left unturned in attempting to achieve that goal.

Sensible management of fisheries is another topic Mick has strong views on. He believes the overnight closing down of the tuna drift net fishing was a mistake. A sledge hammer to break a nut! It was a very good fishery in the sense that it gave the whitefish grounds a break, a chance to recover. A total ban was unnecessary; the situation could easily have been controlled by putting a limit on the number of nets allowed per boat. That is not to say he does not recognise cases where a total shutdown of breeding grounds is sometimes necessary, but he continues:

Nobody knows better than fishermen about where the breeding grounds are and what the stock situation is. They should be consulted and listened to. There's no good closing down breeding grounds when it's too late. The kinds of procedures followed by other counties, Iceland for example, are worth looking at. Some years ago in Sweden I vividly remember seeing massive Icelandic herring being processed. I later learned that the fishery from which they came was closed when the total catch allowed dropped to 4 per cent. The closure allowed stocks to fully recover. As a result the fishery has now been up and running for a number of years. In contrast, as an example, we have continuing nonsense about the coral reef off the south-west of Ireland. While the Marine Institute and other bodies say that they have only recently become aware of its presence, fishermen have known of its existence for years and years. It is, of course, a major breeding ground and one that fishermen have frequently said should be closed down. Has their advice been acted upon? Of course not, instead gill netting, possibly the most harmful kind of fishing on that particular breeding ground is now in full swing. The damaging aspect is that parts of nets break away, especially when hauling in bad weather. Those part nets remain fishing indefinitely, and end up lying at the bottom of the sea with masses of dead fish meshed in them. We pointed out that catastrophic situation to the authorities on numerous occasions but nothing has been done about it. It's simply a matter of no control leading to the decimation of fish stocks.

During his fishing career, it could be said that Mick occasionally sailed close to the wind in every sense of the word. An incident off Dunmore East in the mid-1960s was responsible for making headlines in the national press. In the weeks prior to the incident, tensions were running high between skippers of Republic of Ireland boats and their Northern Ireland counterparts. The scenario seemed to unfold as follows. The southern boats had been fishing and landing herring at Dunmore East for some time before the arrival of the then more modern and efficient northern boats. Not only did the northern skippers have the advantage of superior boats but their fishing gear was also more advanced. As a consequence landings by northern boats were greater and more frequent, sometimes up to three times per day. The southern men were not impressed and became less so when it was known that northern skippers sought to curry favour with buyers, who were frequently acting as agents, by giving sweeteners in the form of so many cran of herring free of charge with each landing. Figures of five to ten free cran with every hundred landed were quoted. That, of course, resulted in a very lucrative situation for the buyer/agent, who in addition to his regular fee and/or profits was also earning handsomely from the sale of free fish. Southern skippers simply couldn't compete. McGrath Brothers, Dunmore East, did stand by southern boats in as far as possible by providing a very limited outlet known as the Fresher

Market. As time progressed, a situation developed where, in a form of protest, irate southern skippers began to dump their fish onto the pier. A reek of herring formed so large that it eventually slipped into the sea. At that stage the northern skippers were in no doubt as to the feelings of the southern men.

Mick's account of developments from there on went as follows:

We, the skippers of a few boats from the west but mainly from the Wexford and Waterford coasts, were up at Mass in Killea on a fine winter's Sunday morning. The church overlooked Dunmore East. Outside the chapel after Mass as we looked out across the bay and the sight of the northern boats fishing made our blood boil. There was no point in us going out because we couldn't sell the fish; there were no takers. We decided there and then that the time had come to take action. We could no longer stand idly by; the northern men were well aware of our dilemma but made no effort to play ball by curtailing the numbers of catches or cutting out the sweetener incentive. The following morning about ten boats, my own *Ardent*, Willie McCarthy's *Orion*, along with Wexford and Dunmore East boats set for Baginbun Bay with the intention of apprehending the northern boats. There were a number of them fishing there at the time. Various heated radio conversations took place as we surrounded them and explained, not too politely it has to said, we had reached the end of the line and that we were going to prevent them from fishing.

As we closed in on the boats there was minor contact between my boat and a 70ft northern boat, the *Victory*, built at Skinner's Yard in Baltimore in the 1940s. What actually happened was the scarf on the bow of the *Victory* got pulled around when she made contact with the band on the port side of my boat. The alleged criminal activities by Republic of Ireland boats at Baginbun Bay were quickly reported to the authorities, so that when we arrived back at Dunmore East later in the day the Garda Síochána were on the pier waiting for us. By then the press had also got hold of the story. One publication headlined it as 'The Battle of Baginbun'. I was accused of being the main protagonist behind the action taken against the northern boats, and of ramming the *Victory*. Later that day I was arrested and taken to Limerick Jail.

It seemed a bit extreme but that's what happened! I was young and I suppose a bit brash with the Garda. My uncle, who had been in the force, tried to advise me to behave. There were two charges brought against me, one of attacking another boat by ramming, the second was that of conspiracy. The cases were tried separately in Dublin over several weeks. The hearing involving 'ramming' took place in the High Court, that of conspiracy in the Central Criminal Court. In the 'ramming' case the plaintiff's attorney brought many witnesses to support the claim. Things were not looking good for me; in fact my senior councillor said as much to me.

I was seriously worried and felt that my councillor was giving up the ghost rather easily. I didn't know what to do. I went out for a walk and ended up looking in shop windows along Henry Street. Suddenly something in one window caught my eye. It was a toy in a cardboard box; a child's set of boats of different sizes. I went inside and bought it. Something told me it could help with my court case. I felt during the hearing that there were times when evidence given was not fully understood, or indeed sometimes misunderstood, because all present were not *au fait* with maritime terms. If I was allowed to use the toy boats in court to demonstrate what happened things could become clearer. That was my thinking anyway. I approached my senior councillor with the idea. His reaction was, if you take those toy boats into court you will be held in contempt. I felt I didn't have a lot to lose; I was prepared to take the chance. When I explained to Judge Kinney that I would like to demonstrate, with the help of the toy boats, exactly what happened when the boats collided at Baginbun Bay he immediately agreed. At the end of the hearing I was found not guilty and I have no doubt the toy boats swung the case in my favour. A conspiracy is usually very difficult to prove and that was so in the second charge brought against me. I was found not guilty.

I will be forever grateful to the South & East Fishermen's Co-op who stood by me during those difficult times. There was no way I could personally have found the money to fight those cases back in 1966. Special mention goes to Mr Laurence Lett, Wexford, without whose financial backing things would have been very different.

The afternoon with Mick had passed by so quickly that I didn't realise just how late it was. Eileen, the lady of the house, insisted that I stay a while

Right: Mick (right) surrounded by friends on Dunmore East pier on his departure for Limerick Jail.

Below: Mick and Eileen on their wedding day.

longer and have a bite to eat. I couldn't help noticing lots of anniversary cards displayed on window sills, sideboards and fireplaces. When I commented on the cards, Mick proudly announced that he and Eileen had just celebrated their fortieth wedding anniversary. It gave me great pleasure to congratulate the obviously still very happy couple. Even though Eileen wasn't happy about standing in for a photo, off she went and arrived back with a picture of herself and Mick cutting the wedding day cake all those years ago. May they have many, many more wedding anniversaries in the years to come!

THROWN IN AT THE DEEP END

HUGH NELSON OF DONAGHADEE, COUNTY DOWN

The surname Nelson is synonymous with seafaring at the County Down coastal town of Donaghadee. Generation after generation of the well-known maritime-orientated family have gone down to the sea, not only in search of livelihoods, but also as prominent volunteer members of local RNLI lifeboat.

While the name of Hugh Nelson had previously been brought to my attention, I hadn't contacted the man. It was a telephone conversation with one of his contemporaries that prompted me to do so. One is never sure how another will respond to a cold telephone call asking for chat to discuss his lifetime experiences. In this case I needn't have worried because Hugh's reply was immediately positive. Subsequently, further cordial telephone conversations with this obviously genial gentleman left me in no doubt that a visit to his Killaughey Road residence at Donaghadee would indeed be a pleasure. So it turned out to be!

Comfortably seated at the Nelson home in a room lavished with seafaring memorabilia and enjoying the hospitality extended by his wife Sylla, I listened as Hugh, now well into retirement, began to enlighten me on his family background. First he reflected on the early years of the 1900s. As with the majority of Donaghadee's male residents of that era, his grand-

Hugh Nelson at Donaghadee, December 2009.

Lucy, 1901.

father William George Nelson was a fisherman. He owned a 20ft yawl, *Lucy*, a boat which took part in a famous lifesaving rescue – so famous that what appears to be a newspaper photograph dated 10 November 1901 is in Hugh's possession. It shows the *Lucy*, her crew, and in the distance, three masts of a stricken sailing vessel.

He related details of the incident as follows:

In 1901, nine years before the first RNLI lifeboat was stationed at Donaghadee, a sailing ship went ashore to the north side of the harbour. The closest lifeboat, a sailing vessel, was based at Groomsport on the north County Down coast at a distance of almost five miles. With great difficulty it was brought to Donaghadee by road, where poor weather conditions prevented it being launched. My grandfather, frustrated by delays in getting a rescue boat to the stricken ship, decided to get his own boat, the *Lucy*, involved. He, with the help of six or seven other men, transported the *Lucy* out along the road to a point where the golf links horse became available. Here they harnessed the animal to the boat and pulled it down over the beach and on to the north side of the bay where the ship had gone ashore. They launched the *Lucy* and went out to the ship, where they boarded it and helped the crew to refloat her. The initiative of my grandfather and the other local men is recognised as having saved the ship and its crew.

When the RNLI decided to station a boat at Donaghadee in 1910, William George Nelson and a few other local men were requested by the institution to travel to England to help choose a suitable boat. As far as Hugh can ascertain, the boat *William & Laura* was the first motor-powered lifeboat on the coast, and certainly the first lifeboat to be based at Donaghadee. The original coxswain unsurprisingly was the same William George, with Hugh's father, also named Hugh, an original crew member. Among the rescues in which the *William & Laura* partook was that of a French vessel and crew. It was a rescue that prompted the French government of the day to present William George with a certificate and a medal, with medals also being presented to all nine remaining crewmen.

Sadly, William George himself was to become victim of poor weather conditions at sea. One day in 1917 he, along with his fourteen-year-old grandson and a second boy of the same age set out to fish at the Copeland Islands off the County Down coast. As it turned out, the sea was too rough to fish so they decided to return to Donaghadee. On approaching the pier a large wave hit the boat and washed William George and the fourteen-year-old boy over the side. His grandson, Davey, rather freakishly escaped drowning and lived to tell the tale. Yet, nothing was known of the tragedy until some time later when the boat was washed ashore. The body of the man who had done so much to save others was recovered from the sea a day later. The body of the young boy was never found.

Hugh's father, Hugh senior, strictly followed the seafaring way of life so closely adhered to by his ancestors. As a young man he spent some years in the merchant service, but as time went on, fishing became the main source of employment. Hugh joined his father as a 'crewman' on the 35ft open yawl *Seven Sisters* on his fourteenth birthday, Friday 6 December, 1946. The significance of the yawl's name becomes clear when one learns that Hugh was one of a family of ten children, seven girls and three boys; all girls born before the boys.

The main types of fishing carried out were that of longlining and harvesting the bivalve molluscs, known as clams. Hugh remembers longlining as being hard and unpleasant work. In order to provide bait, specially made pots or creels were shot (set) along the shore and hauled daily. The pots were designed to catch what were known locally as 'buckies' – large whelks. Hugh's part in the bait preparation was to sit and smash the 'buckie' shells with a mallet. That done, the flesh had to be cut into portions of a size suitable to fit on the hooks. He says, 'It wasn't very nice and it was extremely painful on hands.' Gloves that might have given some protection were not an option in those days. With the longlines baited and taken out to sea, it was a case of daylong shooting and hauling. Hugh recalls that, 'After Christmas the lines could be left out all night because from then on dogfish were not active. That alleviated the problems of other fish caught on the hooks, mainly cod, being eaten by the dogfish.' The amounts of fish landed were comparatively small, with main outlets being local fish shops. As Hugh put it, 'Fish wasn't plentiful; a good day would be three or four boxes. You didn't get any worthwhile money for fish. You were just making a living, no more than that.'

Co-existing with Hugh father's fishing career were his lifeboat interests. Around 1923, he was appointed 2nd coxswain, a position he held until he became coxswain in 1949. At that time he replaced Andy White, who took up the post following the tragic demise of Hugh's grandfather in 1917. Incidentally, during the thirty-two years Andy served as coxswain over eighty lives were saved. Hugh did, however, point out that during the war years (1939-1945) many of the local seagoing men, including his father and Andy White, worked out of Bangor, County Down, piloting conveys in and around Belfast Lough. During Andy's absence, Hugh's uncle Samuel (Sammy) Nelson took over as lifeboat coxswain and in 1941 was awarded the RNLI Bronze Medal for rescuing seven crew from the steamship *Coastville* and nine crew from the steamer *Hope Star* in November and December 1940 respectively.

Perhaps, though, it was the tragic events of 31 January 1953 that brought the Donaghadee lifeboat *Sir Samuel Kelly* and her crew to the fore. On the morning of that fateful day the car ferry *Princess Victoria* left

Seven Sisters with a young Hugh on the right and his uncle Sam on the left.

Stranraer on the 7.45 a.m. routine sailing to Larne. Weather conditions at the time were said to be poor but not sufficiently so as to cause the sailing to be delayed. However, within a matter of hours a fierce storm, with winds reaching over 100 mph swept in from the Atlantic, whipping up abnormally high seas which battered the coasts of western Scotland and Northern Ireland. No fewer than 300 people lost their lives at sea during the storm. The single greatest tragedy befell the *Princess Victoria*. Caught in the teeth of the storm she sank shortly after 2 p.m. with the loss of 133 of its 172 passengers and crew. Hugh, then a twenty-year-old crew member of the Donahgadee lifeboat, recalls the events surrounding the catastrophic incident as follows:

It was Saturday 31 January. During the morning the weather was very rough in the harbour. The yawl, then the 38ft *Sunrise*, needed to be pumped out but the weather conditions prevented us from boarding her. We were getting ready to try again after lunch when the phone rang. I answered it and a newspaper reporter enquired if we knew about the sinking of a car ferry. No, I didn't. I asked my Dad, likewise he hadn't heard. That was the first inkling we had of the unfolding tragedy – news obviously didn't spread as quickly in those days.

Shortly afterwards 'the rocket' then used to page lifeboat crews went off. We made our way to the pier post-haste. Meanwhile my father, the coxswain, was briefed by the local RNLI secretary as to the mission and we slipped *Sir Samuel Kelly*'s mooring shortly after 1 p.m. Weather conditions were very bad. By the time we arrived at Belfast Lough there were a number of merchant ships and at least one trawler searching for survivors. In the weather conditions that prevailed, attempts by ships to take people on board from smaller boats would have been fraught with danger. There was a real possibility of the said smaller boats being dashed to pieces off the sides of larger vessels. The best they could do was to provide shelter from the worst of the seas until we arrived. With the *Sir Samuel Kelly*'s greater manoeuvrability and deck closeness to the water, we were able to take a number of survivors aboard.

Having returned to Donaghadee around 6 p.m., we went out again at 9.30 p.m. This time we rendezvoused with a Fleetwood trawler that had picked up six bodies and one survivor. The only place we could get sufficient shelter to make the transfers from trawler to lifeboat was over at Whitehead on the Antrim coast. We returned to Donaghadee during the night and set out again at 6 a.m. on Sunday morning. It proved to be a gruesome day, as floating bodies began to appear in the water. A boathook was used to bring each one close the side of the lifeboat, where two men lying on the deck reached over and caught limbs or whatever, before other crew members then helped to raise the body from the water. In all, twelve bodies were thus recovered to line the decks. The first body recovered that day was that of a child. That done it – it was a real downer for the crew. We returned to base that night and were not requested to go out on the mission again.

Included in the RNLI history of Donaghadee Lifeboat is the following paragraph, 'A Bronze Medal and the British Empire Medal were awarded to Coxwain Hugh Nelson for the courage, skill and initiative shown during the service to the car ferry *Princess Victoria* which sank during a storm on 31 January 1953. Donaghadee lifeboat saved thirty-one people.'

Further reminders of those awful days in 1953 when the men of Donaghadee showed the valour and selflessness for which all RNLI life-

Sir Samuel Kelly exhibited at the Ulster Folk and Transport Museum.

CREW OF THE SIR SAMUEL KELLY

2nd FEBRUARY 1953

Sammy Herron, John Trimble, Sammy Nelson, Jim Armstrong (rear), Hugh Nelson (coxswain), Alec Nelson, Hugh Nelson, George Lindsay, William Nelson, Frankie Nelson.

Donaghadee lifeboat crew following the *Princess Victoria* tragedy in 1953. The young man fourth from the right is Hugh.

boat crews are known, are to be seen in the form of a plaque at Donaghadee pier, and at the Ulster Folk and Transport Museum, where the lifeboat *Sir Samuel Kelly* has been preserved and is now part of the collection.

In 1953, as already mentioned, Hugh was a mere twenty years old and fishing with his father, Hugh senior, in the *Sunrise*, an open 38ft yawl

Hugh Nelson senior baiting lines, 1953.

Seven Sisters II moored at Donaghadee.

which had replaced the earlier *Seven Sisters*. The younger Hugh didn't know it then, but things were about to change, because a year later, in 1954, his father died. He was, he says, 'thrown in at the deep end with my father dying so quickly'. Nevertheless, he went on to fish the *Sunrise* and also engaged in ferrying passengers to the Copeland Islands during the summer months, a practice that was also ongoing in his father's time.

In 1955, Hugh sold the *Sunrise* and launched into a way of life that would see him fish on fifteen different boats, spend time working in a carpet factory and awhile dredging in Belfast Lough. Of the fifteen boats, he owned six, beginning with the 40ft decked vessel *Ocean Queen* (B33), purchased in 1955, and ending with the Manx boat *Golden Sceptre* (B90) around 1991. In between there was a 50-footer, the *Seven Sisters* (B92), in which his brothers also had an interest, the BIM 50-footer *Ros Ard* (B595), the 56ft *Dee Star* (B219) and the 45ft *Sincerity S*. With those boats Hugh engaged in all the varieties of fishing prevalent on the County Down coast during those years. In addition to trawling, seining, longlining, clams and scallop harvesting, during the summer months his boats were also to be found working from the respective Argyll and Ayrshire ports of Campbeltown and Girvan. Over the years, fishing had its ups and downs, with slack seasons and poor prices occasionally combining to make life difficult.

Of all the boats Hugh owned, perhaps the 56ft *Dee Star* has pride of place, and understandably so, because he had her newly built. In 1974

Sincerity S.

The newly launched *Dee Star.*

he placed the order for his dream boat with the Smith & Hutton Yard at Anstruther, on the east coast of Scotland. But all didn't go according to plan, because the yard was forced to close due to financial difficulties. She was finished off at Arbroath. That in itself was not a problem, but a difficulty arose when a builder's certificate could not be procured. That, apparently, was because of ongoing bankruptcy proceeding against the yard. The crux of the matter was that the government grant for the boat could not be released until the certificate was presented. It left Hugh in a situation where he was paying interest on a bank loan for three years longer that he should have. However, he survived the trauma and successfully fished the *Dee Star* until 1986.

As to the nine boats not owned by Hugh that he fished on, he says, 'On many of them I filled in when for one reason and another regular skippers or owners were unavailable, and I also simply crewed on some of them.' As examples he mentioned that when the dredging job finished in Belfast, he and his friend John Watterson fished a boat called the *Girl Doreen* for another man. He also spoke of fishing out of Portavogie in the Lynas, Coleraine-owned *Brightmoney*. At a later date, Jack Millar, Bangor, called for a helping hand when he first purchased the 1947 Tyrrell-built *Oriole* at Portavogie. By the way, Jack renamed the boat *Golden Oriole* (B299). Another boat he spent a short time on was the *Fair Isle*, owned by Portavogie man James Coffey. Previous to buying the *Ros Ard* from Alex Shaw, Portavogie, Hugh fished on her for a few months. He remembers drift netting for herring during that time. As a further example of how he 'filled in' over the years, he recalls fishing in Jack Millar's *Ros Mor* (B89) while the *Ros Ard* was being re-engined. Then when he sold the *Ros Ard* to Willie Lennon, Portavogie, he stayed on and skippered her – all a little complicated! The journey was by no means over yet, because while the *Dee Star* was in the process of being built, Hugh fished on the 66ft trawler *Be Faithful* (B10), owned by Junior Coffey, Portavogie. In the later years of his varied fishing career Hugh suffered with considerable back trouble. Yet, having sold his own final boat, the *Golden Sceptre*, he did two further fishing stints, one with Killinchy man Malcolm Carter on the *Napier* and a second on the *Berachah* (B14), a 68ft trawler owned by William Kyle of Portavogie.

Now in his seventy-seven year, Hugh, who is in excellent health, is obviously enjoying life. I had a terrific time listening to his recollections and looking through the numerous relevant photographs he had so kindly copied in preparation for my visit.

OUTSTANDING FISHERMEN

ALBERT SWAN AND TOMMY WATSON OF KILLYBEGS, COUNTY DONEGAL

On my Killybegs visits to chat with the now senior fishermen of the port, two names inevitably emerged in the course of conversations, those of Albert Swan and Tommy Watson. Nowhere did the names crop up more frequently than during my lengthy discussions with the legendary James McLeod. Sadly, both men have long gone to their places of rest. Because of their obvious standing in local fishing circles, I decided to research what lay behind the prominence which they attained in their lifetimes. Much of what I discovered came through word of mouth.

Before delving into the achievements of the duo, it is worth spending a moment on the background of Killybegs as a fishing port in the early 1930s. I believe one could safely say it was far from vibrant. Small boats, half-deckers and the likes, engaged in various types of fishing at a level that had not moved forward for decades. Small-scale trawling, longlining, some drift netting and potting were the order of the day. It seemed as if new methods of catching fish were not even on people's minds, and as such the old order would continue. Then, as often happens when change seems most unlikely, or indeed is dreamed of, along came a messiah in the form of James McLeod, who introduced seine netting, otherwise known as fly dragging, to the Donegal coast in 1937. James's ambition, coupled with the fishing acumen of his colleague Francie McCallig, breathed new life into Killybegs fishing. In the years that followed, more and more boats suitable for seine netting were purchased by local owners. Whitefish and herring were subsequently landed in quantities previously unheard of.

Amongst the many outstanding fishermen to emerge from that particular seine-netting era at Killybegs were Albert Swan and Tommy Watson. Without making reference to James McLeod, whose lifetime experiences have elsewhere been recorded in this book, it would not be possible to trace the meteoric rise of Albert and Tommy. Both men did indeed become legendary in fishing circles. Albert, eight years James's junior, began his route to fame as a crew member on his cousin's boat the *Jeanette*. Tommy, on the other hand, joined the crew of James McLeod's *Mairead* whilst in his early teens and went on to become the maestro's most illustrious *protégé*. Indeed, it has been said that he was, in a sense, born with a 'silver spoon' in his mouth, because where fishing was concerned, from the earliest days, not only did Tommy acquire the McLeod craftsmanship, he also acquired the orderly, almost naval, thoroughness attributed to the man. It was a thoroughness for which James McLeod was well known, and this was so well instilled in Tommy that it was to remain with him throughout his fishing career.

Albert was fifteen years Tommy's senior. Obviously he had a head start over the younger man in the fishing stakes. In 1954, at the age of twenty, Tommy acquired his first boat, the *Mairead*, which he purchased from James McLeod. At this stage Albert had been skipper and owner of the *Evening Star* since 1951. Previously he had been co-owner and skipper of the *Maeve*. In later years Albert recalled that the Kilkeel-built *Maeve*, fitted with a 160hp engine, was reckoned 'to be the last word where fishing boats were concerned'. That all was well in Albert's world of fishing can be gleaned from the fact that the total cost of the Irish Sea Fisheries Association-financed *Evening Star* was cleared in one year. Indeed, the story goes that when Albert and another Killybegs man, Martin Moore, took their boats to fish out of Galway, so successful were they that the locals chased them.

With the mid-1950s looming, Albert had become firmly established as a top seine-net fisherman, while Tommy, who had recently taken over the

Tommy Watson, hand on the forestay of the *Mairead*. (Courtesy of Francis Cunningham)

Mairead, was immediately successful. That Albert Swan, like James McLeod, was an ultra-progressive and entrepreneurial fisherman is a fact. Indeed, there is little doubt but that he and James, friends and next-door neighbours at St Catherine's Road, discussed every step of the development that led to the introduction of pelagic trawling locally.

Around 1958, with Albert still fishing the *Evening Star* and Tommy fishing the *Mairead*, a working partnership began to blossom between the two men. By then, in the words of James McLeod, Tommy was widely recognised as, 'An outstanding fisherman, truly brilliant'. It would appear that Tommy had thrived on his early training at the hands of McLeod. He is reputed, by a colleague, to have always had 'the best kept boat in the fleet and never lost a day's fishing in his life for want of gear'.

As the years progressed the two men continued to go from strength to strength. Around 1960, Albert bought the *Christine* and shortly afterwards

Albert smiles for the camera from the wheelhouse of the *Christine*.

Tommy parted company with the *Mairead* in favour of the *Easter Morn*. It was then that the partnership of the two men reached new heights. They became an outstanding pair-trawling duo. However, it was when Tommy replaced the *Easter Morn* with the *Radiance* that the *Christine* and *Radiance* combination became famous in almost every fishing port in Ireland and Britain, and I'm told as far away as Scandinavia. The effectiveness of the boats and their skippers when pair-trawling for herring at that time surpassed all previous recorded landings in this and neighbouring countries.

That the *Christine/Radiance* partnership was so successful is attributable to a number of factors. The widely recognised exceptional fishing acumen and general boat handling of Tommy Watson would appear to be of major importance. Joey Murrin, who fished with him for around twelve years, is quoted as saying, 'Tommy must have been the greatest fisherman ever'. Albert allegedly singled out the fishing gear used as being of vital importance. So vital was it that he and Tommy spent much time in Scandinavia and elsewhere selecting the very best. Not only did they use the best of gear but they always carried plenty of it. That proved to be the case on one occasion while fishing in Broadhaven Bay, County Mayo. The story goes that between them they wrecked six mid-water trawls. With the seventh they filled both boats with herring! It is also true that Albert and Tommy did not rest on their laurels when things were going well but whenever the opportunity presented itself they headed off to Scandinavian fishing ports for the purpose of learning how others mastered mid-water pair-fishing techniques. Neither should it be forgotten that the two men got on exceptionally well together; they enjoyed each other's company and their work. Albert, who was no mean fisherman, was also an excellent business man. Tommy, on the other hand, appeared to be more single-minded about actual fishing and all that entailed. It is said that in spite of high expectations on all aspects of fishing and boat maintenance, crews remained with Tommy for much longer periods than was the norm.

As the saying goes, all good things come to an end. So it was in 1967, when the period of fishing fame for the *Christine/Radiance* double act came to an end. Not so, though, for their owners, who simply moved on to even bigger and better things. Yes, bigger in the form of two new state-of-the-art boats, better in the sense of possibilities for even greater

Tommy's *Radiance* at a Killybegs boat blessing. (Courtesy of Francis Cunningham)

landings. Albert took delivery of the Norwegian built trawler *Mallrin* in 1967 – the first fishing vessel built for an Irish owner in that country. One year later, Tommy did likewise, when he took delivery of the *Sanpaulin*, also built in Norway. In the years that followed the owners and their new boats fished on with even greater success. By then, the technique of pair-trawling, originally introduced to the north-west by James McLeod in conjunction with Willie McCallig and later perfected by the partnership of Albert and Tommy, was firmly established. Boat owners around the coast were to benefit from the trail blazed by the celebrated Killybegs pair. It has been said of Albert that he possessed the admirable quality of helping others succeed. He is reputed to have freely passed on information on technique, and furthermore, when he sussed out good gear in Sweden or elsewhere he willingly ordered more for others who were interested.

Albert's *Mallrin* at the Killybegs boat blessing. (Courtesy of Francis Cunningham)

All the while, Killybegs had developed into a modern, vibrant fishing port. What a transformation had taken place since the arrival of James McLeod in the early 1930s! It's a transformation that was to grow for decades to come. Tank boats capable of landing unheard of volumes of fish were soon to arrive on the scene. As a fishing port, Killybegs achieved the accolade of second only to Peterhead, Scotland.

When the time came for Albert and Tommy to call a halt to seagoing, it was not surprising that one way and another they remained involved with the fishing industry. After all, the immense capacity each man had to undertake challenges was not going to disappear. It may be that Albert was more business orientated than Tommy but each found a niche into which they directed their immense knowledge towards net manufacture. Tommy was to become a director of Bridport-Gundry (Ireland) Ltd, where he joined forces with his original tutor and fellow director James McLeod. Sadly, we will never know what great things Tommy would have gone on to achieve in the world of business because, following a short illness, he departed this life in December 1984. His short but illustrious life ended in his forty-eighth year. His funeral was one of the largest ever seen at Killybegs and was attended by representatives from all facets of the fishing industry. Tommy was popular, highly respected and widely liked for his happy, smiling, easy-going demeanour. Yet, all who knew him in fishing circles were very aware that he had a very serious perception of what fishing was all about.

He will be ever remembered for his part in a very courageous rescue at Dunmore East in 1958. It took place on a particularly stormy February day, 300 yards from the pier. Three boats, Tommy's *Mairead*, Johnny Hickey's *Ros Aoibhinn* and Georgie Buchan's *Jack Buchan* left the pier together. The *Jack Buchan* led the way. At the time, a tide running against what is said to have been 60mph gale had whipped up very high seas and turbulent conditions along the shore and in the vicinity of the pier head. Waves were reported to be at least 20ft high. There are various accounts of what exactly happened to the *Jack Buchan* in the minutes following her departure from the pier but the certainty is that she was hit by a huge wave, capsized, floated bottom up for a short time, and was briefly righted by another wave as she crashed in between two jutting boulders at a place called the Closh. She was smashed to pieces. Skipper Georgie Buchan along with crew members Benny Armstrong, Denis McClafferty, James White and John Byrne, Killybegs men all, drowned. Thanks to the alertness and exceptional boat-handling skills of Tommy Watson in atrocious sea conditions, one crew member of the *Jack Buchan*, John James Lyons, was plucked from the raging seas. He and Benny Armstrong were the only ones on deck when the boat capsized. Tommy manoeuvred the *Mairead* into a position whereby one of his crew members, Pakie Cunningham, was able to throw a rope to the man they spotted holding on to a fish basket whilst floundering amidst the massive undulating waves. He had obviously grabbed the basket as he was washed overboard. Miraculously, John James managed to catch onto the rope thrown by Pakie and was pulled in to safety over the side of the *Mairead*. Pakie's brother Francis, another crew member of the *Jack Buchan*, did not to go on the boat that afternoon as she set out to shelter up river at Waterford. Instead, he decided to travel by car with the intention of later meeting up with his fellow crew members. Alas, it was not to be.

Unlike Tommy Watson, Albert Swan was to live a long life and he certainly made the most of it, by not only engaging in various enterprises but also holding office in several organisations. He loved a challenge! His first involvement with net-making came when the Norwegian firm Syversens, who had taken over the Donegal Carpets factory at Killybegs, diversified into trawl manufacture. That was in the mid-1970s. Albert, who had by then retired from fishing, became managing director of Syversen Trawl Ltd. That led to a link with Willie Jensen of Hirtshals in Denmark, said to be the best trawl maker in Europe. Accordingly, a connection had been established with Hirtshals fishing gear and Ireland, and to Albert's new factory and business, known as Swan Net Ltd. His aim was to specialise in mid-water trawl technology. The company expanded rapidly in Ireland, Britain and further afield, especially in North America and Iceland.

Previous to Albert's adventure into the world of net-making, Bridport-Gundry had in 1968 formed a partnership with James McLeod to open a net-making factory, Bridport-Gundry (Ireland) Ltd at Killybegs. The company established by James, like Swan Net Ltd, thrived and earned a solid reputation at home and overseas. The reputation of the Killybegs-based factories was further enhanced when, in 1999, Swan Net Ltd, took

Francis Cunningham, 2009.

the overall prize in the 'Marketing Campaign' section of the Icelandic Fisheries Awards competition. As a result of the international awareness created by winning this prestigious award, the Hampidjan Group, a powerful Iceland-based concern with interests throughout the world, acquired a shareholding in Swan Net Ltd the following year. In 2002, Grundrys Ltd and Swan Net Ltd came together within the Hampidjan Group to form Swan Net-Gundry Ltd. How fitting it is that the companies founded by next-door neighbours James and Albert now bear the combined names for all to see on the Killybegs seafront.

Albert had many other strings to his bow. To list but a few, he was a founder director of An Bord Iascaigh Mhara, a founder member and later chairman of Donegal Co-operative Fisheries Association, a Killybegs Harbour commissioner and the first Irish skipper to insure his crew against accidental damage.

Of Albert, who lived to be an octogenarian, and Tommy, whose life was cut cruelly short, it has been said that, 'No monument could ever adequately reflect the contribution they made towards building the local community.' Nonetheless, perhaps a reminder at the seafront would not be out of place!

FISHING WAS IN THEIR BLOOD

JOHN LYNCH OF HOWTH, COUNTY DUBLIN

It's a beautiful March morning at Howth. I'm waiting at the West Pier entrance to meet up with John Lynch, who's driving from his home to collect me. Several cars pass by, and then one stops. A glance at the driver tells me to ignore it – that heavily bearded man is not John. Yet, he's signalling me towards the car. Closer inspection reveals that the gentleman in question is indeed John. The explanation is simple; since we last met a year ago he'd decided to grow a beard. As amiable folk go he could easily become a genuine contender for Santa of the year!

A native of Castletownbere, County Cork, John has long been a resident of Howth, County Dublin. It was in 1956, as a seventeen-year-old, that he first set foot on the east-coast port. He arrived as a crewman on the BIM 50-footer *Ros Beara*, a boat owned and skippered by his first cousin, Gerry O'Shea. However, three months later he went back home to Castletownbere where he remained until 1959, when he returned to Howth.

John began his lifetime fishing story by retracing his early years at Castletownbere. It was a story that had a familiar ring to it. A few months previously Gerry O'Shea had told virtually the same tale. That is not surpris-

John Lynch senior keeping his hand in!

ing, because as boys, even though John was ten years Gerry's junior, they both began their fishing careers on the half-decker *Grove*, a boat owned by John's father. John's father and Gerry's mother were brother and sister.

The *Grove* was one of those small versatile fishing boats so familiar around the Irish coastline in the 1930s and '40s; 25ft to 30ft half-deckers fitted with 13/15hp Kelvin engines, a couple of hammocks and cooking facilities that were limited to a primus and a small Jack Tar stove. Of note was the absence of a motorised winch, which meant that all hauling had to be done by hand. They were boats of vital importance to the livelihood of hundreds of families in small and often remote coastal communities. Alas, so-called progress had seen to it that the days of those boats are gone forever.

The seasons more or less dictated which particular kind of fishing John and his uncles engaged in. Scallop dredging was common during the winter months; the warm days and fine weather of summer signalled it was time to put the lobster/crayfish creels aboard, and maybe engage in hand-lining as well. The welcome arrival of harbour herring in early autumn saw four or five nine-score drift nets being prepared. John recalls that when the 'big spawny herring' were first landed in September the wonderful aroma of frying fish filled the air as it wafted from open doorways throughout the town. It was, he said, 'The most beautiful smell of all.'

It was not unknown for the *Grove* to be found as far afield as the Kerry coast in search of lobster/crayfish. With a small yawl on tow for the purpose of doubling the number of creels to around forty, the crew shot (set) and hauled every two hours or so. John recalls that crayfish were plentiful but that prices were poor. Landed fish were for the French market. They were purchased by local agents before being transferred to storage tanks at Crookhaven. From there the live fish were exported in purpose-built tank ships.

John moved from the *Grove* to the *Ros Beara* and fished locally on her for three months previous to that first trip to Howth. There were, he says, 'very few bigger boats engaged in trawling out of Castletownbere at that time. Consequently, fishing grounds around the bays were "fresh" and prime fish such as sole, plaice and turbot were plentiful.' Remoteness from the Dublin fish market and associated transport costs were the main reasons behind the move of the *Ros Beara* from its Castletownbere base to Howth.

By 1956, seining was well established on the Irish coast. With an abundance of whitefish being caught in nearby waters, Howth was buzzing. John recalls:

When we first came here it was all seine netting. There were good enough prices for whiting, up to ten shillings a box on the pier, which meant no transport costs. A day's landing could well total in the region of £100. Of course, then we only fished a five-day week and landed each evening. There have been big changes since I started. I believe all fishermen were happier then. The camaraderie was great and you didn't have to worry about the enormous amounts of money that are now involved with boats, gear and running expenses. When I fished on the *Ros Beara* expenses scarcely reached £50 a week; oil was around a shilling a gallon and food cost no more that £10 or £12.

While the *Ros Beara* was to become very much part and parcel of that scene, John, as already mentioned, returned to Castletownbere to fish with his father. On his return to Howth in 1959 he rejoined the crew of the *Ros Beara*, then skippered by Gerry O'Shea's brother Sean. This time he was to stay. In 1962, he first met the young lady who was to become his wife two years later.

When Sean O'Shea purchased the *Easter Morn* from Tommy Watson at Killybegs in 1963, John joined the crew and fished on her out of the north-west port for a number of months before returning to Howth. He says, 'There was a lot of fish in Donegal Bay then. The trouble was that small as well as mature fish were caught and landed. Loads of young haddock and whiting went to the fishmeal factory. As a result stocks were ruined.'

Back at Howth, he continued his fishing career on the *Silver Harvest*, a 75ft Scotch-built boat, owned by Michael Doran, a man who, like several other fishermen, settled there in the 1950s. The family name is now synonymous with Howth in the form of the well-known retailers Dorans on the Pier. John recalls a number of lucrative herring seasons at Dunmore East on the *Silver Harvest*, a great boat to carry herring, he says.

By 1969 the young Lynch chap who first came to Howth in 1956 had reached the ripe old age of thirty-two. With vast experience in the art of various fishing modes under his belt, he decided to further his career by acquiring his own boat. Purchase of the 1960 French-built, 60ft *John Martin* (D379) fulfilled that goal. She was, he says, 'a great sea boat, beamy, stable, and fitted with a six-month-old 287hp/214kW Baudouin engine. We took 210 cran of herring aboard her one night, that's 840 boxes.' John went on to say that whitefish seining out of Howth at that time was very good; landings of cod and whiting were profitable. Yet, it was the pairing partnership of his boat and the *Jasper*, a boat owned by Johnny O'Connell, Valentia Island, County Kerry, that was particularly successful during herring fishing seasons at Dunmore East in the early to mid-1970s. Alas, a ruling in 1977 was to herald the end of that rewarding period. Herring fishing in the Celtic Sea (that is an area of the Atlantic Ocean off the south coast of Ireland) was terminated for the foreseeable future. It was a measure introduced by the government/Brussels to preserve stocks.

As with many fishermen I have spoken with, John feels that as necessary as the curtailment might have been, it brought with it the end of an era. Not only would herring fishing off the south coast never be the same again, but the manner in which the ban was overseen dented relationships between the fishing industry and the government. A major bone of contention arose during the 'closure period' because of what Irish fishermen saw as discrimination. The problem was that while they were banned from fishing in that particular area, large trawlers, particularly Dutch vessels, continued to do so and landed fish caught at their home ports. It did indeed seem ironic that foreign trawler owners and crews profited at the expense of Irish fishermen. If my memory serves me right, a number of Irish fishermen spent time in prison as a fallout from an infringement of that particular ban. There were further repercussions when the ban was lifted several years later, because as John recalls, 'The markets on the Continent for Irish-caught herring had more or less disappeared, never to be won back again.'

By the early 1980s, the children of John and Cora Lynch, or at least five of the six, were beginning to show a keen interest in boats and fishing. The sole female member had other ideas. Of the boys, John says, 'Fishing was in their blood.' John (junior), Martin, David, Peter and Brendan all served apprenticeships on the *John Martin* under the watchful eye of their father.

In time, John, Peter and Brendan made harvesting the sea their careers, with all three acquiring skipper ticket status. John (junior) temporarily owned his own boat, the 6oft French-built *Oilean Baoi*. While all was going well on the fishing front for the Lynch family, around the corner lay immense sadness. The untimely death in 2003 of Cora, wife and mother, following a prolonged illness, brought untold grief.

During his wife's illness, John senior was obliged to give up fishing. That more or less signalled his retirement, with Peter taking over as skipper of the *John Martin*. Around 2005, a family decision was taken to sell *John Martin* and *Oilean Baoi* and, as it were, put all their eggs in one basket. It was a case of moving with the times by purchasing a larger, steel-hulled, modern boat; a boat capable of engaging in off-shore fishing and remaining at sea for several days if necessary. The smart-looking, French-built, 24m by 4m by 3.4m *Eblana* (D379) fitted the bill nicely. Her previous French owner, a fish factory proprietor, saw to it that the *Eblana* was well laid out and incorporated all modern requirements including ice makers, a freezer and refrigeration. Block frozen prawns sold mostly to Northern Ireland and mainland Europe have a shelf life of up to two years.

Brothers John, Peter and Brendan all fish on the *Eblana*. John, the 'senior skipper', relinquishes that position to the capable hands of Peter when he is required to do so. On the day I visited Howth the boat was fishing off the south coast. On the pier, John senior introduced me to Peter, who was ashore getting gear ready for prawn fishing. I chatted for a while with the extremely affable young man regarding fishing in general. He is obviously happy in his work, but as with all Irish fishermen laments the fact that conditions are not more favourable.

It is a fact that the once thriving fishing port of Howth is now but the palest of shadows of its former glory. For the most part, fish sold locally is imported. John remarked, 'People say to me fish is not the same as it used to be, I reply of course its not because it is not caught in Irish waters, its foreign fish, it comes from places such as the Faroe Islands, Iceland or maybe much further afield.' The few boats that use the harbour do so only because the town is where their owners are living. I asked John what had happened to the port where at one time it was virtually impossible to get a berth at the pier, a pier where boats at times lay five or six abreast.

Eblana at Howth pier.

John hesitated for a moment, because it's hard to know where to start. The bottom line is that there are no longer fish in any quantity to be caught in nearby waters and as a consequence owners have over the years opted out through decommissioning schemes or selling off boats. Life in recent years has become even more difficult for owners due to costly consultancy fees, service and certification in order to comply with statutory boat standard requirements.

But why are fish no longer plentiful in nearby waters? John believes that there are multiple reasons, and he homed in on a few. He lays the blame for the complete absence of whitefish at the doors of the pelagic boats that arrived mainly from the north and cleaned the place out:

Previous to their arrival we used to see cod on the sounder at ten fathoms off the bottom. Our nets would only reach half that height, but we knew that some would drop down for a few days sooner or later and that we would get enough to keep us going. The pelagic boats, on the other hand, with nets [bottom trawls] maybe 15 fathoms high caught all those fish. The nets used were those for catching herring and mackerel and should never have been used for whitefish. There should have been a restriction at a certain net height in order to give fish up-the-water a chance. Those pelagic men seem to want to catch all in one week. The consequences of their actions meant there were no fish left to spawn; slowly but surely the species died out. It was always good here until the pelagic boats came! To make matters worse, when fish were scarce during the summer they went out and fished a twelve-hour day, maybe catching a box or half a box per hour, ending up with six or eight boxes for the day. They kept going until they got every last fish out of it. You just can't do that if stocks are to be maintained! We never did, once fish got scarce in one spot we moved on elsewhere; we always gave fish a chance to make a comeback.

Next John spoke of the travesty he believes the introduction of Intervention brought with it. Also known widely as withdrawal, Intervention was an EC initiative first operated in Ireland in 1976. It was a system that guaranteed prices for fish landed completely independent of market forces and human need – an open invitation to catch and land as much fish as possible regardless of stock depletion or indeed human consumption. In many cases it led to fishermen fishing for withdrawal only. Fish were landed, sometimes in very large quantities, only for the purpose of making money. Had it then been possible to store fish long term we would probably have ended up with a fish mountain comparable to the famous butter mountains of that era. Instead, as John recalls happening at Howth, when boat loads of whiting arrived at the pier a dye was poured on the fish. They were thus rendered useless for human consumption and returned dead to the sea not far from where they were caught. It was, as John says, 'A shocking disregard for stock preservation.'

John also had harsh words about how Spanish, French, Belgian and Dutch trawlers came up the Irish Sea, and as well as wiping out all prime

Peter Lynch with pet Rosie keeping him company on Howth pier.

fish such as plaice and sole, permanently destroyed fishing grounds, including the breeding banks. With regard to the Belgian fishermen, he says:

> They came with their beam trawlers and cleaned all before them. They cer-
> tainly had no traditional rights. How they were allowed to fish here I will
> never know! When I started fishing here there were no Belgian trawlers to
> be seen. The mistakes were made in 1972 when we joined the EU and there
> is no going back now. The foreigners have got our quotas and will never
> give them up. The review currently being discussed is highly unlikely to
> change anything; we will get nothing back from the Spanish or the French.

The issue of foreign boats fishing in 'our waters', is the one topic which never fails to raise the hackles of Irish fishermen. It is easily the most contentious area of all where grievances are concerned. The EU Common Fisheries Policy, coupled with the perceived ineptness of our government to negotiate more favourable terms, has left an indelible mark, one that it seems will long remain in the memories of Irish fishermen attempting to harvest the seas around their own country. John's take on the matter is that the Spaniards have far more 'scope' than they had previously. He says:

> Fish caught by them off the west coast has realised three times the money that Ireland received from the EU … Spain has built up a brand new fleet of trawlers on the back of money made from fish caught in 'our waters'. Quotas and prices are seriously against us. Keeping ahead of the game is no longer an easy matter. The cost of fuel is a major concern, so much so that even a modest rise could easily put a lot of boats out of business. Two years ago, when the price of diesel to fishermen rose to an all-time high, it accounted for nearly half a boat's total running costs. A big part of the remainder went on crew wages and fishing-gear replacement. Gear is very expensive now! Fishermen can't afford to lose money. If you do, you go backwards, and that's no good. What a pity our governments over the years didn't look after the fishing industry better. What you see at the harbour here, or rather the lack of it, is indicative of how badly things have gone. That there is not a good living to be made by fishermen at all coastal ports of this island, surrounded as it is, or was, by premier fisheries, is criminal.

When I asked John if he could recall any particular memories from his fishing days, surprisingly it wasn't anything directly to do with fishing that he spoke of. What immediately came to mind was something that took place while he was still a seventeen-year-old fishing out of Howth on the *Ros Beara*. The year was 1955 and he had 'gathered up a few pounds' so he decided to visit his mother at Castletownbere. On the way, he had to wait a while in Cork for a bus connection and decided to pass the time by walking around Patrick Street. In the window of Dunnes Stores he spotted a beautiful pin-striped suit on a tailor's dummy. He took an immediate fancy to it:

It was the nicest suit I had ever seen and it was the right size for a sixteen or seventeen-year-old. I went into the shop and told the assistant that I wanted the suit on the dummy in the window. He told me that they had similar ones in the shop, but I said, 'No, I want the one in the window.' He brought it out, I stripped off the 'old gear' I was wearing and tried on the suit. It was priced at £7 but it was perfect – I would take it! Encouraged by the assistant, I also purchased a shirt and tie. Feeling really on top of the world I walked out into Patrick Street all dressed up in my new attire. I caught the bus to Castletownbere and got there just after dark. Arriving at my home I knocked at the door. My poor mother, who wasn't expecting me, opened it. She looked at me curiously, as if I were a complete stranger, before asking, 'Who the name of God are you?'

'I'm your son John!' I answered.

'Well, well,' she replied, 'Where did you get those fancy clothes? I have never seen the likes.'

I asked John if he had been happy in his chosen career. His reply was instantly positive:

Fishing was a great job. There was something new every day. It was wonderful to set off in the morning, away to sea, with no traffic or the likes to contend with. It was just a case of wondering where to try the first shot and then waiting to see how much fish was in the net at boarding time. Before shooting again, maybe on the way to a new piece of ground, you could have a chat and a bit of craic with other skippers over the radio. If you liked the job it was great. It was, of course, at a time when half the male population of Howth were employed in fishing. There are very few now! Days on end at sea leading to unsociable working hours has seen to that. The money earned is not sufficient for the effort put in.

On the whole, few people go through life without their share of woe. Where John is concerned it was the death of his wife and the loss of his brother that marked unforgettable periods of anguish. He was fishing out of Dunmore East in December 1968 when news began to filter through that the 63ft MFV *Sea Flower* was missing at sea. It was of immense significance to John because his youngest brother, Bernie, was a crewman on the boat. It was fairly quickly established that the *Sea Flower*, with its crew of five men, had left Kilmackillogue pier in Kenmare Bay on 22 December to return home to Castletownbere. She never arrived. Having struck a rock off Ardgroom in poor weather conditions, the vessel soon became a wreck. She remained intact for some hours, but unfortunately the regular rescue services did not reach the scene in time to save the lives of those on board. Neither did the very brave men who set out from Castletownbere on the fishing trawler *Ard Beara* in what were by then atrocious weather conditions. Having made their way to the scene via the notorious Dursey Sound, their hazardous attempt was in vain. All hands on the *Sea Flower* were lost. Amongst them was Bernie. The other four were Bere Island native Michael Crowley (skipper and John's onetime fellow crewman on the *Ros Beara*), Niall Crilly of Douglas, Cork, Noel Sheehan of Dursey Island and his cousin John Michael Sheehan of Dursey Sound. All bodies were recovered and John recalls the acute grief felt at the sight of the five bodies laid out side by side at a mortuary in Kenmare. The sadness that prevailed during Christmas 1968 at Castletownbere and around the coastline was truly palpable. 'A terrible time of sadness,' John says. John went on to say that Bernie was due to join the crew on his *John Martin* but went on the *Sea Flower* instead. Somehow that reminded him to mention that another brother, Tim, had fished with him for twenty-seven years.

It was well into the afternoon when I took leave of John. Time had passed ever so quickly. Chatting with and listening to a man who has witnessed the whole spectrum of change in Irish commercial sea fishing had been a most interesting experience. His love for fishing and all that entails is obvious. He has concerns for the long-term future of fishing on this island of ours. In particular, he feels that while on one hand our own fishermen are being bureaucratically squeezed out of the industry, on the other hand more and more fish are being imported, some of which are caught in 'our waters'. A calamitous cocktail indeed!

John has a constant reminder of the sea. His home is so situated that looking northwards one is immediately captivated by a rather special Irish Sea vista. Immediately off shore is the uninhabited island of Ireland's Eye, further north is the greater mass of Lambay Island and further still, at a

Ireland's Eye from Howth pier.

John Lynch junior, just back from fishing off the south coast.

distance of 12 or so miles, John pointed out the barley visible form of St Patrick's Island, lying off the north County Dublin coastal town of Skerries.

As I was about to leave, word came through that the *Eblana* would be back in Howth the following morning. That being the case I decided to return. It was then that I met John junior on the pier. Rather like his brother Peter, he was a most affable man who took time to chat with me on the pros and cons of present-day fishing.

THINGS WILL EVEN OUT

TONY FAHERTY OF ROSAVEAL/ARAN ISLANDS, COUNTY GALWAY

I first became acquainted with Tony Faherty in January 2008. He was in search of a copy of BIM 50-footer plans and got in touch to see if I could help. It was my pleasure to do so. Our first face-to-face encounter was at a Galway boat show in February 2009. We arranged to meet at his home at Rosaveal the following Sunday morning. It was a heavenly morning. The distant haze far out in the bay scarcely interfered with the delightful coastal ambience. The stunning rugged beauty of the Galway-Bay-rimmed terrain as I drove west through the Connemara countryside via Barna, Spiddal and Inveran was simply divine. Before I called on Tony, as I do when I visit any fishing port, first I took a look around the pier. There were lots of boats of various dimensions and types on view, most showing signs of recent activity. When I enquired at a local shop as to exactly where Tony's home was located, a lady who was paying for her groceries at the check-out looked up, smiled and said, 'I'm his wife, just follow me.'

Tony's assertion that he had been more a wheeler-dealer that a fisherman surprised me! I knew he came from solid fishing stock on Inis Mor, Aran Islands, and that the Faherty name remains synonymous with fishing.

So what did a man who over the years fished on and owned a series of boats actually mean? Well, he went on to explain that he was twenty-seven years of age when he started fishing. He did go out with his father a few times when he was about sixteen but recurring seasickness proved a serious problem for him.

He embarked on his first business venture in 1966 at the age of twenty. It entailed retailing coal and fertiliser to the residents of Inis Mor. In the first instance his father, John, then owner of the BIM 50-footer *Banrion na Mara,* shipped twelve tons coal across to Kilronan from the mainland in order to get the young entrepreneur up and running. After a time, snags began to surface, the most serious being, as Tony put it, 'There was not money much in it, £1 a ton or something like that, and it was too much bloody hassle.' As any twenty-year-old would do in such circumstances, he landed his father with the business!

However, Tony's entrepreneurial talent was by no means extinguished! Soon he would tap into the fact that oil-powered generators were the only source of electricity on the Aran Islands. Generators had to be maintained and indeed occasionally replaced. So he travelled to England in 1967, where he undertook a crash course on generator instalment and maintenance. Back on the Aran Islands, where he helped keep power and light in supply, he had other irons in the fire, not least his involvement in construction work at Kilronan pier. To that end he recalls providing crushed stone and having six or seven men employed. It was then too that his father bequeathed him the *Little Flower*, a small boat that Tony never fished.

The year 1968 was an eventful one in the lives of the Faherty family. Tony got married, his father sold the *Banrion na Mara* to Achill man Paddy Corrigan, and his brother Des acquired the brand new 56ft *Ard Aluinn*. Des, who was later to become a big-time player on the Irish fishing scene, learnt the business from his father on the *Banrion na Mara*. Tony didn't particularly want to go fishing but with the pier development finished there was no other work available. In 1972, a berth became available in the *Ard Aluinn*. A year later he switched to the 80ft *Azure Sea*, a boat Des had newly built at Killybegs. Tony remembers his years on the *Azure Sea* as extremely lucrative. There was, he says, 'big money made at the herrings in Dunmore East'.

Tony Faherty, 2009.

Better late than never, Tony had embarked on a career that for many years to come would one way or another see him involved with boats and fishing. Following his spell in the *Ard Aluinn* and *Azure Sea*, he returned to the island, sold the *Little Flower* and bought the 36ft *Fintan Bay*. Having fished her for a year or so, in 1976 he 'traded her in' for the Scotch-built 50ft *Village Maid*. It was to be a short relationship, because while fishing her on the east coast the following year he sold her to a Clogherhead man. Next in line came the BIM 50-footer *Ros Ronain*. The *Ros Ronain* was no stranger to Kilronan, as twenty years previously it was there that she found her first homeport under the stewardship of Martin O'Faherty. Tony didn't do a lot of fishing with the *Ros Ronain*, instead he used her as a stand-in for delivering mail and goods to the islands when the regular ferry and cargo boat 'went away'.

In the early 1980s, Tony was involved with what seemed like a plethora of boats and experienced mixed fortunes. While still owner of the *Ros Ronain*, he also had the *Labriscan* and the *Azure Sea*, which he bought from his brother Des. He fished the *Labriscan* himself for a while until the *Azure Sea* came on the scene. While still in his ownership and fishing out of Killybegs, the *Labriscan* filled at water and sank at the pier. Tony continued to fish the *Azure Sea* but a fate similar to that of *Labriscan* was to befall her. He recalls, 'I was getting ready to go to the Porcupine Banks in the *Azure Sea* in 1983 when she filled at Kilronan pier. I didn't fish her anymore after that.'

By then the seismic change that was to revolutionise fishing on the Irish coast had taken place. It was the arrival of Des Faherty's *Atlantean* and her likes, which gave the concept of fishing a whole new meaning for the vast majority of people on our coastline. Up until then, for the most part, when dimensions of boats were quoted, it was feet and inches that were referred to. An 8oft fishing vessel was regarded as big. But now the more convenient metric system was to replace its imperial counterpart as a means of expressing dimensions. The *Atlantean*, built at Maaskant Machinefabriekem, Bruinisse-Steelendam, Holland, in 1981, boasted the following measurements: Length over all, 53.45m; Beam, 9.50m; Draught, 4.70m. That length converts to about 176ft – twice the size of what would previously have been regarded as a large fishing boat.

Tony joined the crew of the *Atlantean* in 1984 and remained on her until 1987. By then, he says, 'Her original length had been increased by 12m. Her carrying capability had been increased from 400 tons to 800 tons.' He went on to say that Des retired from fishing in the mid-1980s and it was then that Killybegs resident and County Mayo man Martin Murphy, who had been mate on the ship, took over as skipper. While he fished on the *Atlantean*, Tony once again speculated and bought the 72ft *Day Dawn II*, a vessel he describes as, 'A great sea boat. I used her trawling for prawns and whitefish.' The wheeler-dealer part of his make-up was indeed ever present and it was not going to change. While he still had the *Day Dawn II*, he bought and sold another boat, the 66ft *Jean Elaine*. Next on his shopping list was the 8oft beamer *Sean Seosamh*. However, on her way to the fishing grounds one morning 'a sleepyhead' allowed her to run ashore.

Azure Sea.

Replica of the MFV *Atlantean*.

Fortunately the crew were rescued. The boat was later brought in and sold on following a refit. Not one to sit around, Tony went off to Peterhead, Scotland and once again invested in a fishing boat. This time it was the 86ft Scotch-built *Shearwater*. With a big demand for prawns in the late 1990s and early 2000s, the *Shearwater* was an ideal boat for fishing the Porcupine Bank, approximately 200 miles west of Ireland. Tony says, 'There was good money in that fishing. You could work with small crews because there was very little tailing of the medium to jumbo prawns being caught. You had only fairly small amounts of good quality whitefish.'

Sadly, ill luck was again to strike a Faherty fishing boat. Tony recalls the scenario as follows:

> The *Shearwater* was a fine boat. On a March day in 2004 she set out for the Porcupine Bank skippered by my son, Desmond. Around 74 miles west of the Aran Islands a fire broke out on board. The cause will never be known. Once the fire got hold, dense smoke made it impossible to go below deck where controls for the generators and the intake and extractor fans were located. It was clear from the outset that boat could not be saved. A mayday message was sent out and the crew quickly began to board the life raft. The heat generated became overpowering in a very short time. Emergency services arrived at the scene and rescued the stricken men. Helicopter observers reported a collapse of the aluminium shelter-deck which was quickly followed by general disintegration. Everything in her burned out. The Irish navy vessel responsible for extinguishing the fire stood by the floating burnt-out shell overnight and the following day. I was receiving instructions from all quarters to the effect that the boat was not to be brought into this port or that. Effectively I was not allowed to bring her ashore. What was to be done with her was the question. The navy vessel that was reportedly to standby until a decision was made had to return to port for some reason or other. During the night the remains of the *Shearwater* disappeared forever. I was very glad because I was getting orders from everywhere not to bring her in. Had she been brought ashore cutting up of the hull would have been a requirement. Imagine the hassle that would cause. As it was, I collected the insurance without getting involved in all sorts of messy business.

Tony's final fling where actual fishing boats were concerned came when he purchased the *Lochtuddy* for his son Desmond. The young man had other ideas about what he wanted to do with his life at that particular time. He decided to tie the boat up and go globetrotting. Tony put a crew in her for a while but she wasn't doing very well, so he decided to sell off the tonnage. At the time of our meeting the *Lochtuddy* was a houseboat at Inis Mor.

When I asked Tony if he had any outstanding memories from his fishing days, he surprised me for the second time that morning by saying, 'I suppose it would be the time spent in jail.'

'What time? What jail?' was my response! He replied:

Well, it came about in 1982 as result of charges relating to what was deemed as illegal fishing. The EU closed herring fishing in the Celtic Sea to all counties. Yes, the Irish boats were banned as were the Dutch, but while the Irish were forced to comply, the Dutch returned and began to fish there. The laughable part was that when the owners of Irish boats brought their grievances to the attention of the appropriate government minister, the response received was that it was alright for the Dutch to fish the Celtic Sea because the gear they were using was so sophisticated that it was not catching herring. Incensed by what was regarded as a nonsensical response, seven Irish boats including my own put to sea and fished beside the Dutch boats. Surprise, surprise, the fish caught was, of course, herring; there was no quantity of other varieties. When the Irish boats returned to Kinsale the owners were arrested and charged with illegal fishing.

Following a court hearing we refused to pay £100 bail and as a result we were sent to prison for eighteen days. Seven skippers went in, five of us stayed. I went on hunger strike for seven days. We were transported from Kinsale to Mountjoy Prison in a yellow bus. Our journey up to Dublin was more like a boys' outing. Members of the security forces who accompanied us were very sympathetic towards us. Alcohol, bolstered by a bottle of brandy (compliments of Mick Orpen on leaving Kinsale), was not in short supply. We did, of course, share the liquor with our minders and when supplies ran low we stopped for replenishment. All went well until we arrived at Mountjoy Prison hours later than arranged. The authorities there were not at all impressed. I believe they were considering not admitting us. That would have been a laugh!

We were treated well enough in Mountjoy Prison except that coffee was not served to inmates. Because of that I went on hunger strike for a week, during which time my total food intake was three glasses of milk per day. I believe the other inmates regarded us as a kind of novelty for a while but when they discovered that all we had to do to get out was to sign a piece of paper, their attitude towards us changed. The Minister of Fisheries hadn't the guts to come in and talk to us. He wrote a note asking us, 'to please be sensible and come out'. Eventually we were allowed out. I'm not sure if we were in for the full eighteen days or not.

In November 2007, Tony and his brother Des turned the clock back, as it were, by bringing their father's 1960s boat, the *Banrion na Mara*, back to Galway Bay. It was merely a sentimental gesture, with no particular plan in mind for her future at that stage.

Before leaving Aras Arann, the Faherty family home in Lower Rosaveal, I asked Tony what future he saw for the fishing industry. He is of the opinion that, 'There is no doubt, fishing will come good again.' He believes that, 'Things will even out.' Where Rosaveal is concerned, he maintains that, 'While there were six or seven boats decommissioned in 2008, better boats will soon replace them.' Nevertheless, he is personally glad to be out of fishing.

BOATYARD MEN

The remaining chapters of this book are devoted to men who played a crucial part in the Irish fishing industry. Up to comparatively recent times, the provision of reliable and well-crafted wooden boats was an ever-present constant where commercial fishing was concerned. Down through the years men who went forth in good weather and in bad to harvest the seas trusted in the capability of boats to bring them back to shore safely. Only those experienced in the drawing up of plans and boat building know exactly what it takes for a vessel to remain seaworthy, and indeed how it will perform when laden with fish in adverse weather conditions. Those men are the 'Boatyard Men'. They take tremendous pride in their skills and workmanship. In recent times I have spoken to two such esteemed gentlemen who spent a lifetime at the coalface of wooden-boat building: John McBride, who began his career at Meevagh in 1939, and Michael O'Boyle, who first graced the Killybegs Boatyard in 1952. A second category of ever-present boatyard men were the marine engineers. In addition to fitting and maintaining fishing-boat engines they also oversaw the fitting and maintenance of vital deck machinery. Recently I had the pleasure of meeting Billy Nolan, one such engineer, at Baltimore, County Cork.

I WAS MAD FOR DANCING

JOHN MCBRIDE OF DOWNINGS AND KILLYBEGS, COUNTY DONEGAL

John McBride has sadly departed this life since I met up with him at Letterkenny in March 2009. He was then eighty-eight years of age and a gentleman in every sense of the word. It is true that he wasn't in the best of health at the time, but nevertheless my attendance at his burial five months later at Killybegs came much sooner than expected.

No sooner had we sat down to chat during our March get together at Letterkenny than he quickly informed me that his real home was at Downings, County Donegal, the place he was born and bred. Indeed, one of his weekly outings entailed a visit to the home place on the north coast. Even though times were often tough, he has fond memories of growing up in a caring neighbourhood. That boys were boys in the north Donegal of the 1920s emerged as John related some of the 'goings on' during his school days! With a broad smile on his face he recalled:

We used to light up in the toilet; one of us would have a few drags and 'nick' the cigarette. Then another boy would come along later, light up the 'nicked' cigarette and have a few drags. That's the way it went until the cigarette was smoked down to the 'butt'.

John McBride, photographed during our meeting in March 2009.

John continued:

> My father, a cooper by trade, was born in the mountainous area of north
> Donegal. He used to make barrels and tubs for use in the fishing industry.
> Twice a year he went off to work at herring stations in places such as the Isle
> of Man, and Mallig on the west coast of Scotland. The herring girls would
> gut the fish and place them in layers, belly up, in the barrels. My father scat-
> tered salt on each layer. That was a specialised job, because if too much or
> too little salt was used the fish would not be fit for human consumption.
> When each barrel was full, my father, who was very good at his job, had to
> fit on the lid, making sure the barrel was sealed.

John began his shipwright apprenticeship at the Meevagh Boatyard, Co
Donegal in 1939. The yard was originally a Congested Board of Ireland

initiative but ownership had filtered down via the Department of Fisheries and Rural Industries to the Irish Sea Fisheries Association by the time John joined the workforce. The foreman was Scotchman Jack Buchan. John recalls:

> While I was serving my time I was often transferred to different places on the Irish coastline. Wherever work needed to be done to boats, I was sent. I once spent nine months in Galway. Then I returned to Meevagh only to be sent off again, maybe to Dingle, or to Paddy the Cope's boats over in Dungloe. Most of the work I did was repair jobs. I travelled a terrible lot. It was hard work – cruel at times. I mostly worked outside, often in poor weather conditions, and on vessels lying in mud. Once when I was working at a boat in Galway, the whole beach was covered in frost; you could walk on the sea water. It was so cold that I fainted on the deck of a boat.

John also talked about the difficulty of travelling from one place to another in the early 1940s. For example, he remembers that getting from Downings to Dingle by bus or train, or indeed a combination of both, took at least a week. He laughed heartily as he told of an 'expedition' to Dingle in the company of his foreman, Jack Buchan. 'I'll never forget it,' he says. He went on to relate the story:

> We lost our way at some point and crossed the border into Northern Ireland. We were getting on a train but I had no passport, so along came a customs officer and took me to an office. I had to empty my pockets and show what little I had to the officers present. The train was held up over the head of me. Buchan, afraid I was to be detained, was outside on the platform shouting, 'I hope they are not going to keep my apprentice'. The passengers in the train were splitting their sides laughing at him. Eventually the officers let me go and I got back on the train.

On another occasion he remembers arriving in Tralee on his way to Dingle only to spend a whole week stranded there because there was a problem with getting a connection to his destination.

Somehow in the midst of his work and travels John found time to socialise. He was very keen on dancing. The modes of transport to dance venues in Donegal in those days were shank's pony or bicycle. John was amongst the privileged ones – he had a bike! As such, he thought nothing of heading off for Culdaff, where his sister lived, or maybe the hall at Milford. He described one journey as follows:

> I cycled from Downings to Rathmullan and crossed over to Fahan on a ferry (a half-decker) owned by a man named John Browne. The tide was out when we arrived at the slipway so the passengers had to step into the water and walk ashore. Because there were women and children aboard I took off my shoes and socks, rolled up my trousers and lifted the women and children over. Having put the shoes and socks back on I cycled to Buncrana where I had a bottle of Guinness and a sandwich in McLaughlin's pub. From there I completed the trip to Culdaff via Carndonagh. My sister was delighted to see me. Straight away I asked her if there was any dance in the neighbourhood that night. I was mad for dancing! She said there was, but it was a 'dear one', a supper dance. 'Will you go?' says I. 'Indeed I will if you pay the way,' came the reply. Off we went and I danced the whole night. My day's cycling hadn't taken a feather out of me.

An addendum to that story was that when he arrived back home two days later, a brand new previously ordered brown suit was waiting for him at the local tailor's. John was so pleased with the new suit he felt he had to go somewhere, 'I jumped on the bike and headed down for Milford Hall. There I met a woman, and do you know where I landed with her? Over at Glenveagh Castle.' I asked him if he took her on the bar of his bicycle, but he said, 'No! She had her own bike.' John arrived back home the following morning as his mother was putting out the ashes. 'What woman kept you out all night?', she asked. John never spoke; he ran into the house, divested himself of the new suit, pulled on his work clothes, took a piece of homemade bread from the cupboard, jumped on the bike and headed off for the boatyard. He was fifteen minutes late. Jack Buchan, the foreman, was not amused!

Now let's return to more serious facets of John's early life. As we talked on he remembered that while he was still an apprentice, Jack Buchan retired. Jack didn't want to go but he was an old man at that stage and was given no option. He was replaced as foreman by Arklow man and renowned naval architect James (Jim) Stafford. The ill-fated fishing boat *Jack Buchan* was the last boat to be built under Jack's supervision. She was in fact completed under the stewardship of Jim Stafford. Sadly, the boat's skipper, Jack's son Georgie, and four of his crew lost their lives in that devastating tragedy at Dunmore East, County Waterford. It was on New Year's Day 1958 that the *Jack Buchan* and five other boats left Killybegs for the lucrative herring fishing grounds off Dunmore East. During Monday 10 February, a severe south-east gale blew up, prompting boat skippers to swap the then largely unsheltered pier at Dunmore East for the safety of the upriver Waterford dockside. The *Jack Buchan*, in the company of another Killybegs boat, the *Mairead*, set out from the pier. With the boats less than 300 yards off shore, onlookers were stunned to see the *Jack Buchan* upended by a massive wave. As she turned turtle her keel showed for a short time before she was smashed into the rocks. There were two crew survivors; one who stayed ashore to drive a car to Waterford, and another who was rescued thanks to the exceptional boat handling skills of Tommy Watson, skipper of the *Mairead*, and the alertness of his crew.

Following the completion of the *Jack Buchan* in the mid-1940s, the Irish Sea Fisheries Association decided to close the boatyard at Meevagh, and open a yard at Killybegs. Jim Stafford was appointed foreman and six of the workforce from Meevagh, including John McBride, were transferred to get the place 'up and running'. In addition to John, the men transferred were John McClafferty, Hughie Carr, Eddie Duffy, Eneas (Neety) McClafferty and Denis Doherty. Marine engineer Barney McLaughlin also moved to Killybegs. Shipwrights were in very short supply, which resulted in a number of older men who had previously worked in the Industrial School Boatyard at Killybegs being re-employed. John recalls that, 'Paddy Gallagher, who ran the old boatyard, and Charlie Green, who must have been over seventy years of age, were taken on.'

The first boat built at the Killybegs Irish Sea Fisheries Association Yard, and issued in July 1948, was the 38ft *Girl Claire*. Her first home port was Loughshinney. In February of the following year, at a cost of £2,870, the 36ft *Naomh Cait* came down the slipway and headed for Cahirciveen.

In May 1949, the 50ft *Uncle Pat*, built for the Hickey family of Arklow was launched. Between 1949 and 1955 inclusive, only 50-footers were built at Killybegs. There were nineteen in all launched during that period. Two further 50-footers, the *St John* and the *Taobh a'Ghleanna*, were built in 1959. In the intervening years several boats including the *Ard Macha*, the *Girl Eileen*, the *St Catherine*, the *Ard Chluain* and the *Twilight Star* were built at the Killybegs Yard.

As had been the case at Meevagh, John was again sent out from Killybegs to do jobs at various ports around the coast. In addition to returning to ports already mentioned, he recalls working at Bantry on the Fastnet Fisheries boats and at Schull on Dan Griffins's boat, possibly the *Resolution*.

A grievance that John had about working away from home was that his wages remained the same as those employees who stayed put. He believed that he had become a victim of his own competence; he was sent out because there was no need for a foreman to go with him. He said, 'I was fit to do my work and make decisions without supervision; that was not the case with other men.' Somewhere along the line John was offered the position of foreman at the Dingle Boatyard but declined on the grounds that he and his family preferred to live at Killybegs.

John remembers Jim Stafford as:

A first-class man, very calm, and a nice fellow. When Jim moved on, an Aberdeen man by the surname of Penmann was appointed foreman. He brought a more Scotch style to the yard. Jim Stafford had more of a Jack Tyrrell style, though I believe that Stafford could make a nicer model of a boat.

Around 1952, when the Irish Sea Fisheries Association became An Bord Iascaigh Mhara (BIM), the Meevagh Boatyard was reopened. Neety McClafferty, who was one of the six to move from Meevagh to Killybegs in the late 1940s, returned to Meevagh as foreman. Several boats were subsequently built there. Neety remained foreman until BIM closed the yard. Later it operated under private ownership for a number of years, with Downings man Anton McBride as foreman. John believes that, 'Anton oversaw the building of the biggest wooden boat in Ireland.' I haven't been able to confirm that particular claim.

As John talked he recalled that the first boats built at Meevagh were made from larch on oak. The larch came from Galway. When it ran out euroka was used. He also talked about a boat called the *Elsie Mable* that he worked on at Dingle. She was, he said, 'The only double-framed boat I came across in my time. There were two inches between the timbers. I don't know why. Maybe they were thinking that if they put the two together the seam would rot between them.'

Amongst the esteemed fishermen he recalls are inevitably Albert Swan and James McLeod. They were, he says, 'Legends and marvellous men. You could write a book on their achievements.' But he did go on to say that, 'Killybegs had so many skilled and able fishermen at that time, you only have to think about the likes of the McCallig brothers, Tommy Watson and the Moores.'

As my afternoon of chatting with John wore on, it became clear that his memories were very much echoes of the past. So much had changed during his lifetime. The fact that the 1940s and '50s do really belong to another era was powerfully reinforced. Perhaps, though, what came through more than anything was John's modesty. I was well aware from independent sources that he had been recognised as a shipwright extraordinaire, not only in Donegal but at many Irish seaports, especially on the west and south coasts. But John's wizardry with wood didn't end with boat building, because he was equally proficient in other forms of carpentry such as door, window and furniture making. Sadly, people of John's vintage and natural ability are now very thin on the ground.

Throughout the time I spent with him he scarcely drew breath. He obviously enjoyed talking about the 'old days'. What a pleasant and interesting gentleman he was.

DOWN ON THE SHORE WITH THE HOOKER

MICHAEL O'BOYLE OF KILLYBEGS, COUNTY DONEGAL

Michael O'Boyle contributed significantly to the Irish fishing industry by helping to build boats that went forth to harvest the seas. Now, in what I believe could best be described as semi-retirement, he lives at his residence at Old Road, Mountcharles, County Donegal in the company of Mary, his wife. It was there that I first caught up with him in January 2009. So good was the craic and hospitality that I have been back on many occasions since. My description of his retirement status emanates from the fact that while he is officially retired, he is still extremely active and very much involved with boat building and all that entails.

Michael began his career at the Killybegs BIM Boatyard, County Donegal. As with all coastal towns and villages of Ireland in the early 1950s, employment choices were limited. For the most part, girls there joined the carpet-factory workforce, while young men went on the fishing boats, emigrated to England, or became boatyard apprentices. Michael O'Boyle opted for the last of these choices when on 4 February 1952 he signed the dotted line. As he put it, 'I was a greenhorn going into serve my time, but was very lucky to have senior men of the calibre of John McBride, John McGilloway and a number of other very good shipwrights in the yard.' At a time when working in a boatyard was far from easy, it was of vital importance to have able, committed and decent men take you under their wings. In the early months of employment, the norm for apprentices was to do little more than make tea and the likes. Michael recalls, gratefully, 'I got away from that scene fairly quickly.' He went on to say, 'A fine Killybegs man and a great shipwright, the late Charlie Conaghan was in charge in those days. He was a number one man in every way; a great man on history and all that. He wrote books on it.' With smile on his face Michael added, 'If you were one of his boys, you were one of his boys! It didn't matter if you went out and robbed a bank. As long as you got away with it Charlie would look after you. He was a man before his time.' Michael recalls:

> I went on doing whatever I was told to do during my five-year apprentice-ship. Along the way my main mentor, John McBride, refused the opportunity to go to the Dingle BIM Boatyard as foreman. That turned out well for me because I spent a lot of time in the evenings and on Saturdays repairing small boats and stuff like that with him. He had wonderful hands; he could do any-thing with wood. It was great for me, I was learning all the time.

Obviously Michael was ambitious from the beginning. He lost no oppor-tunity in tapping into John's talents and learning from them. In addition to his boat-building expertise, John made and fitted sash windows and doors. He also made tables and chairs, as indeed did Michael, from bits of oak left over in the yard. Michael did similar extracurricular work with John McGilloway, another great father-figure at the yard. 'Like John McBride, he always kept you on the right track,' says Michael.

As his apprenticeship progressed, Michael was moved from the yard floor to the loft to take part in what is described as 'lofting'. He initially worked with a very able man, John McCahill. When John moved on to BIM Head Office, Michael continued with 'lofting'. Moving from the floor to the loft was widely recognised as a real starting point. Very few got there! Reading between the lines, I believe that when an individual was promoted to 'lofting' it was a clear recognition of talent and ability beyond that of run-of-the-mill shipwrights.

So what went on in the loft, or indeed what is 'lofting'? Well, the loft of a boatyard was a first-floor open space with more or less equivalent dimensions to that of the boat-building area on the ground floor. The loft was where laying off was carried out. The term 'laying off' referred to one of the most vital elements in boat building. It involved the making of moulds or patterns to the exact specifications as shown on the architect's plans or drawings for a particular boat. The importance of the exactness cannot be overstated. When finished, the moulds were passed down to the yard floor and used as templates for the cutting of the various pieces of timber used in the boat's construction. Consequentially, any mistake at the laying off stage resulted in untold problems and may have had to be redone at considerable cost in terms of time and wasted materials.

According to Michael, laying off was a great education in boat building, 'You had the boat on the loft floor before you actually sent the moulds down to the yard. Your heart was in your mouth, of course, in case anything was wrong, especially with a first design.' The job of lofting was so particular that occasionally tea break, dinner or indeed the end of the day had to be ignored should you be in the middle of putting down measurements or lines – you had to finish off the job. It was crucial to make a fresh start every time. Over the years Michael was involved in the laying off of boats ranging in length from 26ft to 70ft.

Michael also spoke of BIM employee and distinguished naval architect, the late James (Jim) Stafford. Jim drew up plans for BIM boats of all sizes. He had been Charlie Conaghan's managerial predecessor at the Killybegs Boatyard. Michael had this to say:

> Jim was always there, keeping an eye on what was going on. Everything had to be meticulously done as shown on his plans. He was a very quite man and a great tradesman, but he would spoil you. You had to consult him on every little detail. He wouldn't allow you to go ahead and do the job on your own; it was as if he didn't trust you. It was a failing in him. I suppose he could be regarded as a poor delegator. That tended to hold you back. Otherwise, he was indeed a perfect gentleman, and his drawings were absolutely brilliant.

Michael went on to say, 'Charlie Conaghan was a different man. He would give you a job and let you get on with it. He was confident that you knew what you were doing.'

As Michael reflected on his days at the boatyard, he commented that, 'Times were tough. Every man walked or cycled to work. You cycled only when you eventually scraped up enough money to buy a bicycle.'

A point in time came when Michael thought of moving on from the Killybegs Boatyard. By then he had met and married Mary. Indeed, it was when he was working at a boat that Mary first came on the scene. The story as told by Michael went as follows:

> I was sent out by Charlie Conaghan to do a job on a boat at a house near Lough Eske. There happened to be a couple of young ladies working there at the time. I needed a bit of assistance to hold a light and one of the ladies offered her services. As it happened by the time she arrived I had the light hung up, so she wasn't needed.

With a huge smile on his face and in spite of minor protests from Mary, he continued, 'Nevertheless she hung around, and to make a long story short things developed from there.'

In 1967, Michael planned to take up employment at a boatyard in Malahide, County Dublin. Somehow BIM got wind of his plans, possibly through his great friend John McCahill, who by then had moved to Head Office in Dublin. Within days he was approached by John with the offer of foreman's position at Dingle. Michael was keen enough, and having discussed the matter with Mary, he decided to accept.

Michael returned to Killybegs two years later to replace the long-serving Charlie Conaghan, who had reached retirement age. Some years later Michael was to return to the Dingle Yard. This time he stayed until 1976, when he once again returned to the Killybegs Yard. Following the sale of Killybegs Boatyard by BIM (*c.*1979), Michael remained an employee in a surveying capacity for some time.

However, his yearning for boat building led to early retirement. In truth, surveying was no job for a man who had spent a lifetime to date steeped in every imaginable aspect of boat construction. On one occasion when there was no other suitable location to build, he opted for the roofspace of the family residence. The keel and planking for a 20ft open boat were manipulated long-ways through an open living-room window and passed through a doorway leading into the hallway. From there they were angled upwards through a trapdoor leading to the roofspace. Thereafter, night in, night out, for the duration of the construction, Mary and the children endured muffled sounds and the tapping of hammers coming from the upper region of the house. With the boat built how was it to be got out? What he did, as one does, was knock a great hole in the gable end of the bungalow. 'Sure there's a window there now,' he says, as Mary rolls her eyes to heaven.

Michael continued to build boats. First it was the angler *Martin Og*, and then came the Galway hooker *Sandpiper*. The boat, property of Lynn Temple, Donegal, is the only hooker ever to be built in County Donegal and has been highly acclaimed by experts on that type of vessel. During the building, which took place on a nearby shore side, a somewhat refined lady had occasion to call on the O'Boyle home in search of Michael. Mary answered the door and responded to the lady's request by saying, 'Ah, sure he down on the shore with that hooker, but I'll give you directions.' The lady, obviously taken aback by what she had just heard, asked if was alright to go down. 'Ah, yes no problem, he won't mind,' Mary replied. She wasn't to learn until later in the day, when Michael returned from his boat building, that the lady had not been *au fait* with the particular type of hooker he was involved with.

I suppose one could say that the greatest challenge to Michael's all-round talent was yet to come. The chance spotting of an advertisement in a local fishing newspaper was the catalyst. A syndicate at Tralee, County Kerry, planned to have a replica built of the nineteeth-century sailing ship *Jeanie Johnston*. The requirement as advertised was for a suitably qualified person to source and oversee the building of one of the most ambitious maritime heritage projects ever undertaken in Ireland. The criteria included the assembly a suitable workforce and the sourcing of all materials required to complete the project. It was an enormous undertaking for which only recognised wooden-boat builders need apply; men with considerable managerial experience and a proven depth of maritime knowledge. The building of the remarkable wooden tall ship would be a massive and complex undertaking.

Undaunted, the former Killybegs BIM employee put his name in the hat. Not surprisingly, Michael, the modest but highly respected and experienced shipwright, was the successful applicant. He was to be the man responsible for the building of a ship whose dimensions were: length extreme, 45m (148ft); length overall, 37.5m (123ft); beam, 8m (26ft); draft, 4.2m (14ft); displacement, 510 tonnes and rig, three-masted barque, with four-square sails/mast, and single topsails.

Michael says, 'Getting a competent workforce together was the initial and main priority.' During his years at Dingle he became acquainted with the superb workmanship, genius and all-round shipwright acumen of the O'Regan family – John and his sons Ciaran and Peter. It was to the younger men that he turned for the cornerstone of the workforce. As Michael put it, 'I knew that if I had Ciaran and Peter on board that all things were possible.' Fortunately, they did come on board and Michael was able to turn his attention to other aspects of the job, a major part of which was procuring suitable wood for the various parts of the ship. That particular search took him, among other places, to Alpine slopes where on sight he identified the exact trees required.

Other facets to occupy him, some of which took him across the water, were finding suitably large saws to cut the huge frame parts, the planks, masts and booms. Also to be procured were suitable sails, rigging, nails and bolts, none of which were readily available. All of this was going on while the workforce was assembling and Peter O'Regan busied himself with the almost impossible task of breathing new life into old, tired and rusted band saws and other items of machinery. That work was going on in a shed at Blennerville, Tralee, County Kerry, adjacent to the open-air site where the building of the *Jeanie Johnson* would take place. An interesting fact is that nationals of eleven different countries were present in the eventual workforce. Michael's son Martin, who worked on the project, recalls the experience as a highlight of his young life. Friendships were forged and opportunities opened up that otherwise would not have been possible.

Under the watchful eyes of Michael and Ciaran O'Regan, bit by bit, the great ship slowly but surely became a reality. There were many hitches along the way; too many to mention here. The important thing is that the *Jeanie Johnston* was launched via pontoon into the inlet at Blennerville in 2002. The dream was realised in 2003 when she sailed from Fenit, County

The magnificent *Jeanie Johnston*.

Kerry, to the USA and Canada. She later returned to Ireland having stopped at over twenty ports in five different countries.

The ship, which now operates as a Sail Training Vessel, a Famine History Museum and a corporate entertainment venue, has proved to be a remarkably seaworthy vessel. She is in every respect a credit to all involved in her construction, but special plaudits have to go to the unassuming and modest Michael O'Boyle. Firstly, it took a man of courage, with confidence in his own ability, to undertake such a daunting and mammoth project. Secondly, the methodical and professional manner in which he conducted his business throughout was exemplary. His judgement in all aspects of the undertaking further reinforced what a great job he did.

I should mention that each time he spoke about what was involved in the *Jeanie Johnston* project he referred back to the O'Regan brothers and their invaluable input, 'Once I had them with me I knew I would be alright.'

Michael's sons Martin and Michael are keen oarsmen and as such they set about building their own boat. Under the watchful eye of Michael, over

Happy Days! Michael O'Boyle (right) and the late John McBride.

a period of two years or so, the 19ft lake boat slowly but surely took shape. On completion the young men decided on a charity row. I'm not certain about this detail but I believe it was Michael who suggested that they should row the River Shannon. The idea came to fruition in July/August 2008, when the brothers rowed over a two-week period from the Erne Estuary at Ballyshannon, County Donegal to the Shannon Estuary below Limerick – 371 kilometres. They raised a whopping €24,200 for charity.

It is worthy of note that not only were they the first Donegal men to row the full length of the River Shannon, but quite simply they are the first and only rowers ever to do so. It was an especially pleasing achievement in the light of having built the boat themselves.

My meeting with Michael went on for longer than expected. I could have listened to his story much longer, but it was getting late. When leaving the O'Boyle home on that January night, I asked Michael what he was up to at the moment. Now, why wasn't I surprised when he replied, 'Ah, pottering around with a boat up in Martin's.'

A BUSY MAN

BILLY NOLAN OF BALTIMORE, COUNTY CORK

Billy Nolan, the boy I grew up with in the West Cork village of Baltimore, County Cork in the 1940s and '50s, went on to become an integral part of BIM's boatyard personnel on the Irish coast. Yet, it was not to boat building that he contributed, but to the sector relating to machinery, including engines, winches, generators, pumps and so on.

With a matter of months separating us in terms of age, it is not surprising that Billy and I sat side by side in the same class at Baltimore National School. We were further bonded through a first cousin relationship; our mothers were sisters. One of the saddest happenings in my young life was the sudden death of Billy's father. It occurred on a beautiful April evening in 1945. He was, at the time, Mechanic of the Baltimore Lifeboat. Throughout the 1940s, RNLI lifeboats stationed within the Rosslare to Galway coastline came to the Industrial School Boatyard at Baltimore for refurbishment. It was while Billy's father, Louis Nolan, was helping with hand-winching a particular lifeboat into the boatyard shed that he collapsed and died. The incident shocked and greatly saddened the entire local community.

Following three years at technical college, Billy began his working career at the Henry Skinner & Sons Boatyard. In 1953, as an apprentice, he joined the marine engineering business of Denis O'Driscoll, The Cove, Baltimore. It was a business that undertook the fitting, repair and mainte-nance needs of fishing-boat engines in ports extending from Kinsale to Castletownbere, and occasionally beyond. It is true to say that for many years, when engines and spare parts were virtually impossible to get, the proprietor, Denis O'Driscoll, virtually singlehandedly kept hundreds of fishermen at sea. He seemed to be at their beck and call when an engine broke down or an overhaul was needed. Scarcity of parts frequently required him to improvise in order to get a boat back fishing as quickly as possible. Improvisation of that kind was often slow and tedious. It called for superior metalwork skills and that with limited materials and tools available.

It was in such an environment that Billy began a five-year apprentice-ship that later led to what was to become his lifetime career. He now recalls being thrown in at the deep end and left to get on with it. Yet, for all that, he deeply appreciates the grounding and experience afforded to him by his employer. Describing Denis, Billy says:

> As with most people Denis had his moments of vexation, irritation and occasional exasperation, but through and though he was good enough and I appreciate the training and vast experience received during my apprentice-ship. We overhauled and worked at fishing-boat engines of all makes and kinds. It certainly stood to me in later life.

Billy's first apprenticeship experience was to assist in the complete over-haul of the *Joanna Mary's* (D214) 88hp Kelvin diesel engine. Worthy of note is that the 55ft, 1941, Tyrrell-built MFV *Joanna Mary*, then owned by Mickey O'Donaghue, Bantry, still visits ports around the coast during the summer months. I wonder if she is still powered by that same Kelvin engine! Billy went on to say:

> At the time, the bulk of work carried out by O'Driscoll's centred on engines of long-line, mackerel and lobster boats that fished out of Baltimore in large numbers. The boats, ranging in length from around 20ft to 40ft and mainly powered by 6/7, 13/15 and 26/30hp petrol/paraffin Kelvin

engines came from Cape Clear, Sherkin Island, Heir Island, Long Island, Schull, Crookhaven, Castletownsend and Union Hall. The *Shamrock*, owned by Mick O'Sullivan, affectionately known as 'Mick the Shamrock', of Long Island, was one of those boats.

Mention of the *Shamrock* had us reflecting on memorable stories associated with her, ones we had heard from childhood. Previous to having an engine fitted in the 1930s, she was reputed as being one of the fasted boats around – the one that came first at all regattas! I suppose you could say the acclaim that surrounded her in those days still exists, because even though she has long been beached and in a state of considerable dereliction, nevertheless a group interested in the maritime history of West Cork decided to take her measurements and hull shapings with a view to duplication.

Other boats and owners of that era that came to Billy's mind included: Denis Den O'Sullivan's *St Veronica*; Dinny Griffen's *Togo*; Willie O'Regan's *St Dominick*; Jack Brien's *Sultan Star*; Willie McCarthy's *Mystical Rose*; Tade Regan's *Mary Kate*; Danny O'Driscoll's *St Michael*; Mikey Harrington's *Ebenezer*; Kieran Cotter's *Heber*; John Beamish's *Marie*; Pat and John Cadogan's *Inane*; Flor Driscoll's *Naomh Fionan*; Joe O'Driscoll's *Carbery Lass*; Michael Donoghue's *St Patrick*; the Nolans' *Florence*, *Hopeful*, *Happy Home*, *Vorrey* and *Dun Aine*; the Deasys' *Gannet*, *St Peter*, *Marian*, *St Finbarr* and *Richard*. The list went on and on, but those recalled give an indication of fleet magnitude and indeed of the number of engines in circulation, each of which needed at least occasional attention.

However, as time went by, drift net mackerel fishing and longlining died away and with them the boats that were engaged in that particular kind of fishing. The 13/15 and 26/30hp petrol/paraffin engines virtually disappeared from the scene, with Kelvin, Gardner and other makes of diesel engines becoming the order of the day. As the 1950s wore on, engines of BIM-built boats provided most business for the O'Driscoll workshop. The level of repair work gradually diminished. In its place came the fitting and maintenance of modern and more reliable engines. Billy believes that diesel engines were much simpler to work on than the petrol/paraffin variety.

By the time Billy had completed his apprenticeship, the BIM Boatyard at Baltimore was well established. Coincidentally, the position of Marine

Engineer at the yard was about to become vacant. Encouraged by the incumbent engineer and by Gordon Knox, a one-time Kelvin service engineer, Billy applied for the post. Gordon, Billy recalled, first came to Baltimore from Scotland in 1950 to deal with an engine problem encountered by Dan Griffin's then brand new *Ros Guill* whilst on delivery from Banff, Scotland. For whatever reason, he stayed on and joined BIM. An interview chaired by the same Gordon at the West Cork Hotel, Skibbereen, in 1958 resulted in Billy's appointment to the post. It was a position he was to hold until BIM interest in the Baltimore Yard ceased in 1979.

In the period extending from 1958 to 1960 inclusive, there were no fewer that nine 50-footers built at the Baltimore BIM Boatyard. The larger part of Billy's work during those years involved machinery fitting, includ-

Billy relaxing at his Baltimore home, 2009.

All that remained of the Baltimore BIM Boatyard in 2007.

ing that of engines. With that done, each element had to be seen to be operating to the optimum before boats took to the high seas. There were, of course, occasions when for one reason or another hard-worked engines broke down. Those happenings required Billy to travel to ports on the Cork and Kerry coasts in order to carry out necessary repairs.

The boatyard continued to be extremely busy between 1960 and 1979, during which time around eighty vessels ranging in length from 26ft to 86ft were built. That averages out at over four boats per year, all of which were required to have machinery fitted and tested. Billy was a busy man! When I asked about the makes of main engines fitted I was amazed to learn of the varieties that were used: Callesen, Caterpillar, Volvo Penta, Cummins, S-Werkpoor, Grenaa, Poyaud, Baudouin and others that seemed to have superseded the more familiar Kelvin and Gardner names. Winches, too, had become enormously complicated pieces of machinery. Billy actually spent time in Norway familiarising himself with the details and workings of one particular type of winch. He also recalls building generator units at the Baltimore Yard from whence they were transported to Killybegs. There the generators were lifted aboard boats and dropped onto prepared beds.

In spite of a busy workload at Baltimore, Billy was occasionally requested to fill in at the Killybegs and Dingle Boatyards as and when the need arose. Recently I mentioned his name to former BIM Area Officer John Murrin and to former Killybegs Boatyard foreman Michael O'Boyle, and both men spoke of him in glowing terms. I asked Billy about his recollections of such assignments. At first he laughed, then he told me of one occasion when he did a two-month stint at Killybegs. During the stay he spent day after day, all alone, fitting a new engine in a big boat. Working alone at such a big job was, of course, bordering on the impossible. However, he carried on; the Bord provided the engine and Billy but no other manpower. Apparently the root of this lay with a difference of opinion between BIM and the boat owner.

He recalled another occasion when working in Dingle. Unknown to him, a dispute of some kind was ongoing at the yard. While it in no way involved him or his work, someone whispered in his ear that it might be better if he stayed away. 'No problem,' said Billy, who hopped into in his car and headed for home.

He did, however, have special reason to recall a meeting that took place on another visit to Dingle when filling in for the regular engineer, Albert (Alby) Collins, who was off at the time with an injury. They met one evening for a general chat and as time went on their conversation drifted to tragic happenings on an October night in 1918. Billy knew little of those events, even though his aunts were directly involved, because the tragedy was rarely ever spoken of at home. I believe secrecy of that nature was symptomatic of the times; children were not told about unpleasant family matters. The account Alby related to Billy of what had happened all those years ago went as follows.

A new Gardner engine had been fitted to the Tyrrell-built, 60ft, MFV *Thomas Joseph* at Baltimore. On the evening of 10 October 1918 it was decided to have a trial run from Baltimore to Schull. In all, fourteen people went on the boat from Baltimore. Among them were Alby, his sister Rita, and Billy's aunts Lily and Nan Shipsey. Apparently it was Nan's thirteenth birthday and because of that she was allowed to go on the trip accompanied by her fifteen-year-old sister Lily and friend Rita. At Schull, three of the people who set out from Baltimore decided to travel back by road. Accordingly there were eleven people, including Billy's aunts, Alby and his sister on the boat during the return trip. They set out from Schull around 9 p.m. By then the weather had deteriorated somewhat; a stiff south-easterly breeze was said to have sprung up. Tragedy struck as the boat made its way in darkness towards the north-west entrance to Baltimore Harbour. She ran ashore on the Catalogue Rocks close to Sherkin Island and sank. Six of the eleven people on board lost their lives. One of those was Billy's aunt Lily and another was Alby's fifteen-year-old sister Rita. Billy's other aunt, thirteen-year-old Nan Shipsey, miraculously escaped drowning. The *Skibbereen Eagle* of 12 October 1918 describes how Alby twice brought his sister and Lily Shipsey to the comparative safety of rocks but they were evidently unable to hold on and were washed away to drown. The Coroner stated, 'Too much praise can not be given to the rescuers of the five people saved, especially to John Harte of Heir Island, who displayed wonderful bravery.' It was a sombre discussion that took place between the two men at Dingle.

Billy continued to work for BIM, whom he described as, 'fine employers', until the Bord's interest in the Baltimore Yard terminated in 1979.

The entrance to Baltimore Harbour.

However, the yard did not close, as a small number of its employees formed a company with the aim of carrying on with boat building and related work. Billy, who retained his interest in the machinery side of the business, became a director. He recalls that, 'The 80ft *Sandra Patricia*, whose first home port was Kilmore Quay, was completed under the stewardship of the newly formed company.' In the years that followed, a number of boats, including those of the steel-built variety, were finished off at the yard. Among those vessels were Kincasslagh man Fergal Doherty's 90ft *Oilean Croine* and Tom Ferguson's Skerries-based 120ft *Sean Pol*.

Sadly, unspecified problems led to the company folding in 1983. For all intents and purposes that was the end of a boatyard that had first been established as part of the Fisheries School, mainly through the efforts of one Fr Charles Davis PP, a legendary priest of Rath parish in the late 1880s. In his article 'Baltimore Fishery Schools' Boat building Activity' Tim Cadogan states, 'The extension of an existing shed and slipway in 1898 enabled the school to commence its first commercial boat building contract, a commission by the Congested Districts Board for the building of a boat for delivery to Galway.' With the boatyard closed, Billy continued to independently serve the mechanical needs of fishing and pleasure craft for several years to come.

Now, along with his wife, Miriam, and family, he lives in glorious retirement at their superbly situated residence overlooking the idyllic panoramic vista of Baltimore Harbour. Indeed, as I sat there I reflected on other evenings of yesteryear, when familiarity and dismissive youthfulness allowed the beauty of it all to pass me by. I do, however, have lasting memories of lying with friends on the grassy bank that then overlooked the piers – 'old and new'. The 'bank', long since developed to form a manicured concrete and stone creation, was a well-established socialising area, where current topics, frivolous and otherwise, were discussed. Out across the harbour we kept a skywards eye on what resembled a great golden ball. It was, of course, the sun, slowly but surely lowering itself behind the striking outline of Sherkin Island. All the while the same sun illuminated the distant but unmistakable towering crags of Gabriel. Those were the days!